REFLECTIONS IN THE NILE

An unpackaged tour from
Cairo to Aswan

by June Emerson

Illustrated
by Jackie Shayler-Webb

KAF BREWIN BOOKS

First Published in October 1987
by K.A.F. Brewin Books, Studley, Warwickshire.

ISBN 0 947731 33 4

Cover design by Mike Hill Studio, Stratford-on-Avon
from original photographs by June Emerson

Typeset in Baskerville 11 on 12 pt by
Litho Link Limited, Welshpool, Powys

Printed and bound in Great Britain
by The Camelot Press, Southampton

DEDICATION

To my husband, whose impossible behaviour led me to discover the joys of solitary travel..........

.......and of coming home.

CHAPTER 1

The gloomy corridor was fenced down the centre, and we were herded along between the railings like sheep, while rows of dusky figures in turbans and long robes leaned over staring and shouting. I would not have been surprised if they had pinched our flesh or poked at us with sticks. This was Cairo airport 'arrivals' section. The flight had landed at 7.30 p.m. and already it was pitch dark.

It all began early in 1984. Britain was in the grip of the miners' strike, and every news bulletin carried the clamour of discontented voices and stories of aggression. I had been reading 'Slow Boats to China' by Gavin Young:

An Egyptian on a bicycle pedalled up to the curb and said, 'You are Holiday Hotel, waiting for ship?'

'Yes,' I said, 'waiting.'

'You want anything?' He leaned closer over his handlebars. 'Some joy?'

'Not now.'

'Okay, maybe later.' He pedalled away. I was surprised by the politeness of it all.

This brief passage, illustrating the Egyptians' gentle acceptance of life's misfortunes, suddenly made me want to drop everything and travel to Egypt.

There seemed little point in making the journey if I couldn't speak to anyone, so I contacted Leeds University to try to find someone who could teach me some Arabic. They put me in touch with a young Egyptian professor who was doing a two-year exchange in this country and who would probably welcome the extra work. Abdul and his wife Sara welcomed me into their home and did their best to teach me not only Arabic, but a great many things about life in Egypt. One day Abdul said shyly:

'When you go to Egypt, will you take something there for me?'

'Yes, of course, if it isn't too enormous.'

'Maybe a sewing machine?'

My heart sank. I was travelling light, and had planned to take a knapsack weighing only eight pounds. The addition of such a heavy item would be a nuisance. Abdul noticed my hesitation and went on to say:

'Not a very big one. Then when we go home at the end of this year there will be not so much to carry. We will have the baby then also.' Sara was expecting her first baby in just a few weeks' time, and the thought of moving the whole flat-full of furniture and a new-born child all the way back to Egypt made me agree to help. As it turned out it was not a sewing machine after all but a portable typewriter that they asked me to take, which was not so bad.

When the time for the journey came, they arranged for me to stay for the first night with Sara's family in Cairo. In spite of all they had told me about Egypt, Cairo airport was still something of a shock.

Amongst the shouting crowd behind the railings I noticed a dark skinned grizzled old man with a white turban and long brown robe looking particularly keenly at me. He shouted what sounded like my name:

'Madaam Jon! Madaam Jon!' It was Sara's father. He shook my hand vigorously, but couldn't speak any English. He waved at a young man in western dress who turned out to be Sara's brother Ali, who spoke quite good English. Ali went off to round up two more brothers who had been posted to look out for me and when we had all shaken hands, we piled into a battered estate car. Ahmed, the eldest brother, drove much too fast through the darkness, tooting the horn continuously. A road-mending machine ground out in front of us from a side street and then stopped, blocking the way with a cliff of steel. Sandwiched between the two brothers in the back, I gripped the seat. With screeching brakes Ahmed managed to avoid it, and skidding in the loose gravel, tore off again.

Hoardings shone with advertisements for Coca Cola and Schweppes, recognisable even in Arabic script. It was just like the road from any other airport until the streets suddenly became narrow and dim. Men in small groups sat at tables under the dusty trees playing backgammon or smoking hookahs, looking like sepia illustrations from an ancient book. We swerved through some more roadworks, dodged round a few piles of stones, and bounced into a rubble-strewn cul-de-sac. Ahmed skidded to a halt, and there was silence. In the shadows stood tenement blocks of assorted sizes, mostly three or four storeys high, with racks of washing standing at the doors or hanging from the balconies. Hardly any light showed from the shuttered windows. It was like one of those awful 'no escape' moments from a film.

We climbed two flights of broken concrete steps littered with refuse and chicken bones. Smiling faces appeared shyly at warmly lit doorways on every landing. At the top I was shown into a living room, lit by a circular fluorescent light. Blinking in the brightness I was introduced to Sara's mother, Zeinab. She was beautiful, but had tired eyes. She wore a long flowered robe, and a white headcloth which gave her face a nun-like serenity. She hugged and kissed me in welcome and everyone smiled and said proudly 'Sara's Mama!'.

I glanced round. This was the living room of a family with six children. It measured about eight feet by twelve and had a padded divan on three sides, with turquoise covers patterned with gold roses. In the centre of the room was a small plastic-topped table. Against the end wall was a bookcase with a television set on the centre shelf, and a few books and manuals on the upper shelves—*and that was all.*

Everything was newly painted. They had only been living there a short while, having been forced to move because, as Ali told me later, their previous flat had fallen down. On the wall was a highly coloured photo of Ali's betrothal and a calendar with a picture of a mosque.

I heard footsteps on the stairs, and a tap at the door. A pale girl of about twelve, with long straight hair, slipped shyly into the room. Her huge dark eyes lit up when she smiled. She was followed by a little girl with brown wavy 'English' hair, who skipped in on bare feet, smiled shyly and hid herself in the folds of Zeinab's dress. Then came a boy of seventeen or so, with a small, newly-nurtured moustache. Another lad of perhaps twenty came last, and everyone was smiling and sometimes cautiously trying a word or two of English.

'Good Morning!' said a confident fourteen-year-old girl who sailed in last. These were all members of the uncle's family from the floor below. We sat round on the divans and looked curiously at each other while the brothers told again and again the story of how they had found me at the airport.

Amal, the eldest of Sara's sisters, brought tea, black and sweet in small glasses.

'You speak Arabic?' asked Ali, presuming, with a smile, that I didn't.

I screwed up my courage, searched around desperately in my memory and said:

'Kilmiteen, wi bass!' This not only means 'Two words, and no more!'

but is also the name of a regular discussion programme on Cairo Radio, which Abdul had told me about during one of my lessons in Leeds.

The whole family burst into delighted laughter and rocked about slapping each other on the shoulders. Amal, completely helpless with giggles, covered her face and buried it in her mother's shoulder. I looked round rather bemused. I knew my Arabic wasn't brilliant, but didn't think it was that funny.

'You have made us so happy', Ali explained, wiping his eyes.

I thanked them, in careful Arabic, for their happiness and Amal's face almost exploded. She leapt to her feet, pointed to me, then to the light on the ceiling and bubbled out a phrase which Ali explained meant 'You are like a light that has come to our house.' From that moment I was one of the family, and all shyness had disappeared.

When I told them that, back in England, Sara was well, and that the baby which was due in about two weeks was very active, her mother and father went silent. Father, now in just his long brown robe and white crocheted skull cap, bent his head and, elbows on the table, drummed his fingers on his brow. They were all worried about Sara as she lost her first baby after only four months of pregnancy. Zeinab herself had lost six children. They sighed, and Aunt, who by this time had come upstairs to see what was going on, said quietly 'Ilhamdu Lillaah' ('It is God's will'). I heard a cock crow outside in the darkness.

The mood soon cheered, for there was a Charlie Chaplin film on the television, and we rocked about with shared hilarity, language problems forgotten.

At about 11 o'clock Zeinab prepared a huge supper of omelettes, salad, little bean-curd fritters, brown pitta-bread, vegetables in a savoury sauce, white feta cheese and jam. Dish after dish was brought in from the little kitchen. When everything was laid out there was some urgent whispering, and Amal went back to the kitchen and returned, looking confused, with a knife and a fork. She didn't know quite what to do with them, and poked them nervously amongst the dishes.

Ali and I were the only ones eating, he with his fingers, and I, watched with fascination by the family, with the knife and fork. We had more sweet black tea, and they also produced Evian water which they had bought specially for me.

One by one the children from downstairs slipped away, with a smiling goodnight. They were such easy-going, loving, relaxed people who moved around each other without collisions. It was not surprising that Sara longed to be back with them after her two years in Leeds.

I was given a large bedroom to myself, and the rest of the family dispersed mysteriously into the small flat. The bed was huge, big enough for three people, with a long flat bolster, blankets and a quilt. The family had decided that I couldn't possibly move on to a hotel the next day, but must stay for three or four days—for as long as I wanted. This was to be my home.

The shuttered window of my room led to a tiny balcony. The street was dark with just a few single bulbs on the buildings making pools of dim light. The racks of washing hung in the warm darkness, barely moving in the breeze. There was an occasional bark. It looked like a stage-set; and I couldn't believe that it was real. The cock crowed again.

CHAPTER 2

My bed was hard, but comfortable. I slept peacefully, until into my dreams came the sound of a man singing—a strong, natural voice rising in a curving phrase and then falling. He was echoed distantly by the same phrase, and the song lapped away into the sky like ripples on a lake. It was 5 a.m. and the muezzin were calling the faithful to prayer from minarets all over the city. I wanted them to sing for ever with their strong assurance.

Much later I got up. For breakfast I was offered two hard boiled eggs, pitta-bread, omelette, cold potato chips, jam, feta cheese.

I washed my hair, and it dried quickly as I sat on the balcony in the sun with Amal and Zeinab. We watched the street. Some small children were kicking a misshapen ball around amongst the sand, rubble and parked cars, several of which had padded covers tied over them in an attempt to keep out the sand. A tabby cat curled up on the cover of the car below, licking its paws in the sunshine, looking so English that I wondered what language it spoke. Neighbouring balconies were hung with a fascinating assortment of surplus chairs, wicker cages, sacks, bunches of garlic, round-bellied pots and baskets. The street gradually came to life as shutters were opened and dark faces popped out to view the day. Quilts were thrown over balconies, radios were turned on full blast, carpets were shaken. An ancient man in a white robe and turban shuffled through the dust of the street with an enormous white clay pot on his shoulder, calling as he went. He was a honey seller, and was summoned from a high balcony by a big man in striped pyjamas who had been stretching and scratching himself.

'You are honey!' bubbled Amal, pointing at me and laughing with delight at her timely and accurate English.

Later in the morning Ali and I walked to the bus stop. I had to go into the city to call at the police headquarters, the Mugamma, in Tahrir Square to have my passport stamped. This must be done by law during the first week of any visit. There was so much to see on the way and it was all so different from home that it made me dizzy. Everywhere people were selling things, not only from shops and stalls, but from hand-carts, cardboard boxes and heaps on the pavement. Old women in long black dresses and head shawls sat cross-legged on the dusty ground surrounded by mounds of watercress piled on newspapers. A mountain of golden loofahs wobbled on a cart as it was trundled along the uneven ground. Another squatting figure guarded a row of wicker cages containing doves, and three or four perched on top making no attempt to fly away. A passing housewife bought a few and they made no protest as she popped them into her shopping basket and balanced it on her head. A man crouched down by a small fire on the pavement, roasting sweetcorn on a grid, and he fanned the glowing charcoal with a bird's wing. Men sat on the ground in groups talking and here and there a solitary figure could be seen squatting or leaning against a dusty tree, looking at nothing in particular.

The buses that passed were bursting with people bulging out of the doors, and some were hanging on by one hand. I didn't see how we could board any of them, but Ali hurled himself energetically into one and pulled me in behind him. There was a framework of hand-rails fixed to the ceiling, but I was too squashed to reach up to it. Almost as soon as we were on board a charming man gave me his seat, and I pressed myself in next to a bulky woman in black who turned round to flash a gold-trimmed smile. To my surprise there was no unpleasant smell of closely packed humanity, presumably due to the ritual washing before prayer five times a day. The crowd chatted and laughed as the bus slowly ground its way, hooting all the time, through the solid traffic to the centre of the city.

Outside the Mugamma, which is a massive curved grey building, skinny little soldiers wearing huge boots and holding machine guns stood guard. Inside, the gloomy corridors teemed with people. A shoe-shiner ran his business in a passage on the first floor. With remarkably little delay my passport was stamped, and I got a big smile and a 'Happy New Year'.

The traffic seemed to make up its own rules as it streamed noisily round, particularly at junctions, and traffic-lights only seemed to fuel the competitive spirit. A friend had told me that in Cairo, red means that you *can* go, and green that you *must* go. At one junction a small policeman was desperately haranguing the writhing mass of metal through a megaphone.

'What is he saying?' I asked Ali.

'He is asking them to observe the rules,' answered Ali. That must qualify for the Guinness Book of Records as one of the most useless jobs on earth. To add to the problems, pedestrians tended to walk in the road as the pavements were thick with sand, rubble, boulders, concrete blocks, chunks of steel cable and other such hazards. They are building an underground railway system in Cairo and consequently the roads are in a terrible state.

'In a hundred year, Cairo like London!' said Ali, proudly optimistic. I thought this one of the saddest prospects imaginable.

Although there is litter everywhere, it gets broken down and absorbed into the sand which seems to have a sterilising effect. What will happen when 'progress' changes the litter from mostly paper, as it is at present, to plastic is a sobering thought. We saw street-cleaners bent double collecting it into small rush baskets, some using a small hand-brush but many used just their bare hands.

Our throats were dry, so we stopped by a large galvanised water tank standing on the pavement in which floated a two-foot block of ice and several bottles of Coke. Ali took two out and a lanky lad flipped off the tops for us. We were not expected to pay until we had finished drinking.

We walked on to find the British Embassy (closed as it was Sunday) and then went over the Tahrir Bridge to Gezira Island and up the Cairo Tower which is 590 feet high. The only time I heard silence that day was in the lift. Tense silence. The view from the top would have been fantastic, but a haze of sand hung over the city and we couldn't see far, just the western-style tower blocks of the city centre, interspersed with dusty palms, and bisected by the great gleaming river. In comparison with the yellow brown dust everywhere the sight of the Nile has such impact as almost to quench your thirst. My eyes kept turning urgently back to it.

We passed several mosques as we wandered through the city. Behind some of them were brightly coloured tents, hung with lanterns, beautifully carpeted and containing rows of high backed gilt chairs. Here the dead are brought in their coffins, draped with rugs or quilts, for their friends to come and mourn them before they are taken outside the city to be buried in the graveyards on the edge of the desert. We saw two coffins, each borne by about six people, who had to weave through the traffic and negotiate their load without being mown down.

We travelled back on the train, which was much quicker than the bus. It was full to the doors, which were left open and people hung on to the handles by one hand or sat on the steps dangling their legs. The engine was festooned with small boys having a free ride. The fare for the five mile journey was about 2p.

After another huge meal I slept for an hour or two. Zeinab feeds people whenever they appear, according to their personal timetables, so it is rare for more than two to eat together. When we finish eating, Ali summons any available female to clear away, fetch him water, make tea and clean the table. He was quietly regal and the womenfolk were very amiable about it.

In the evening Ali took me to Maryland, which is a modern pleasure park. We sat beside a stagnant pool illuminated by coloured plastic parasol-lights, drinking tea and talking about our respective ways of life until it grew cold. He, like all the other brothers, wants to come to England to work, and couldn't understand at all when I tried to explain that there would be no work available. London is their Mecca.

As we walked home I reflected on how difficult it is to 'read' people of another race. One glance at someone in England tells you a lot about them: the way they dress, their style of shoes, the way they stand or walk. Hear them say a word or two and you know a whole lot more. Here *everybody* is an unknown quantity. We passed a Coptic church and Ali wanted to know whether it was unlocked. He approached a man who, in the darkness, looked as if he was wearing a dead cat on his head. To me he definitely seemed to be the wrong person to ask, but he proved to be very helpful. The church was locked but he showed us where we could go to see some murals in the courtyard at the back. We passed some people living in a shelter made of bricks on a building site. The men sat round the brazier warming their hands and talking, two women were huddled in the warm glow of candle-light shining out from the pile of bricks. Were they poor, guarding the building site, or just squatters? I never found out.

CHAPTER 3

I hardly heard the muezzin cry that 'Prayer is better than sleep' the next morning. While I tackled the usual enormous breakfast there was a knock at the door and a little bird-like woman popped her head in. On her head was balanced a pile of flat loaves. She went through to the kitchen and gave most of the loaves to Zeinab, who came to introduce her to me.

'Om Saabir,' she said, pointing at her neighbour. Om Saabir, two loaves still wobbling on her head, began to babble excitedly at me. I looked blank, so she leaned nearer and shouted louder, her parrot-squawk voice almost piercing my ear drum. I thought it was only the British abroad who considered that volume increased understanding. Leaning towards her I cupped my hand behind my ear as if I was deaf, and grinned at her. Zeinab shrieked with delighted laughter—it seems that Om Saabir is famous for her volume. Still squawking Om Saabir shook my hand, and then went off down the stairs. We were friends.

Ali took me into the city to telephone home, and we went by train this time. Some farm ladies with big aluminium pans of soft white feta cheese were in our carriage, going in to market. Several passengers were quick to help them off the train at Rameses Station and hoist what must have been well over 50 lbs weight on to their heads. Some of the women carried the cheese in wicker baskets, and as they walked the whey dripped down on to their shoulders.

Rameses Station was busy, as it is the main railway station in Cairo.

'The trouble in Egypt—no discipline,' confided Ali, gesturing towards the crowds pouring in through the 'Exit Only.' We found the telephone office where there was the inevitable queue, and rows of people sitting on chairs looking at nothing. Your position in an Egyptian queue is not according to who is there first, but whose need is the most urgent. After standing around for a while, Ali went to the front of the queue and handed in a slip of paper with my home number on it, together with the international dialling code. The assistant took it, and within minutes we were directed to one of the row of booths along the wall to take the call.

There was no reply. Momentarily homesick I went to the newspaper stall to look for an English paper, but the Times cost £1.50, and was several days old, so I didn't bother to buy it.

After this we went to Thomas Cook's in Tahrir Square. I wanted some information about small hotels in the towns further down the Nile, as the sources I had tried in England had not been very helpful, being mainly geared to group tours. I had also failed to get hold of my friend Nick, a record round-the-world cyclist who has done the Nile on his bike. This was a pity as there was so much he could have told me. When Cook's realised that I didn't want to be Cook's Toured they lost interest and weren't terribly helpful. I was also surprised to find that, had I bought tickets there, they wouldn't have accepted a credit card.

We passed the Mugamma again, and I learned something interesting from Ali about the little soldiers with the big boots: their machine guns have no ammunition.

'Then why the guns?'

Ali shrugged. 'Maybe could use to hit?'

The bus home was crowded as usual, but I was invited to share the driver's area together with a massive woman and her baby. The traffic was wild as usual with a sort of controlled cheerful competitive spirit, when not at a complete standstill. It was a long, tiring ride. Whenever we came back from a trip into town we were coated with a layer of sand. My shirt collar developed a thick brown rim in half a day. When we arrived home I had a shower. The bathroom is tiled and has a lavatory, wash basin and a shower. The mixer tap for the shower is at waist-level and disgorges directly on to the floor, and the water runs out through the drain in one corner. When you use the shower itself it sprays the whole room, which makes the toilet paper completely unusable, but as Egyptians don't use the stuff it doesn't matter to them. In the bowl of the lavatory is a narrow curved tube pointing upwards. This is linked to a tap on the wall which, when turned on, sprays the necessary parts with cold water. I was glad I'd remembered to pack toilet paper.

After supper Ali went to see the new year in with his fiancée at her parent's home. They are betrothed, but their marriage cannot take place until all the goods and furniture for their new home have been bought, right down to the last teaspoon. This is the way Egyptian Muslims do things.

After he had gone, Amal and her cousin Hussein were delighted to have me to themselves, and hauled me out to sit on the balcony in the dark and watch the street. We drank tea and cracked roasted melon seeds, spitting the husks over the edge. Armed with my vocab. book we had crazy giggly conversations.

At 7.30 Hussein took me to the local telephone headquarters, about a mile away, to try to 'phone home again. We were told to wait 1½ hours for a free line. Hussein was prepared to sit and wait, but I persuaded him to show me round the district, so we wandered the streets like a couple of teenagers; cracking nuts, chewing gum, looking in shop windows and going all round a late-opening supermarket translating the names of things to each other. Back to the telephone, and after another half-hour wait I got through and had a fleeting three minutes to talk to my family. (This cost £7.)

We rambled around a bit more ending up at Maryland again for tea by the pool. When we got home Hussein took me downstairs to see his family's home, proudly showing me every room. The flat was dark, crowded with furniture and smelled a bit stale compared to upstairs. Aneesa, Hussein's mother, probably can't get around to do the housework easily as she is massive, but massive. We sat on the divan in the sitting room and Hussein's father Yusef, much to my surprise, brought us coffee and cakes.

Another mystery was solved for me today. When I had called for my lessons in Leeds I was sometimes startled to find Abdul and Sara in their night clothes. It seems that Egyptians wear what appear to be night-clothes all the time when they are in the house. Men in the long gallabiya or sometimes pyjamas, and women in what would be called nightdresses in England. When they go out the men add a head cloth, turban or scarf, although many of the young ones wear western clothes. The older women put on long dark street dresses to go out, often black. Many of the young girls now wear modern western dress, but keep their limbs and necks well covered. On the train I saw a school group in which all the girls were veiled. Far from concealing their beauty, the light blue cloth drew attention to their enormous brown eyes, making them intensely attractive.

We all saw the New Year in together in the downstairs Sawys' flat. There was no ceremony or anything corresponding to Auld Lang Syne (which I felt quite unable to translate into Arabic, so I kept quiet about it.) We just wished each other a Happy New Year and drank tea together. The family were overwhelmingly loving. They wanted me to come every year, and to bring my whole family with me. Invitations for trips and meals kept coming and it was getting difficult to think about breaking away, but a lot more of Egypt lay beckoning to the south. At the end of the evening I said firmly that I would be going on to Fayoum on Thursday.

CHAPTER 4

New Year's Day began with a little hazy cloud in the sky, but the sun soon came through. After breakfast Zeinab, Amal and I had tea on the balcony and Father, Muhammed, went off to work. Up to that morning, whenever I had seen Muhammed, he had worn traditional Arab dress which made him look wise and dignified, but going to work in the local supermarket he wore a white jacket and grey trousers and looked like a tired old man. Muhammed calls Zeinab 'Asal', which means 'Honey'. Zeinab, although she works so hard, is always ready for a chat and a joke. She is roundish, but not as fat as many Egyptian women, and is extremely supple, in fact all the Egyptians seemed to be double-jointed which made their movements a joy to watch. Although she had a gas cooker and modern cupboards in her kitchen she would squat down in the old Arab syle to grind and mix things on the floor with pestle and mortar. Amal (Amal means 'moon') is about 18, tall and slim with huge brown eyes. She laughed most of the time non-stop, particularly when I tried to speak in Arabic.

Selim, the boy next door (son of Om Saabir) is a student of agricultural science at Al Azhar University. He had offered to take me out for the day. While we were having our tea he came over and gave me a poem which he had written:

When you comed to me
I'm forgit every things
I'm forgit smile the moon
I'm forgit my silf
Because I rimimber
You sweetly smile.

If I forgit you
I'm forgit my life
I don't forgit you for ever
Because I love you

When you camed to me
The stars cames whith you to me
When I see you
I see the moon
When I see you I see the moon

I see every things so sweetly
I see the moon but
I don't feeling by it

'All people in our street love you,' he added, seriously. 'If the ground not carry you, we carry you in our heads, in our eyes, in our heart.'

At this the big lady in the balcony opposite called out Happy New Year, and said that she loved me too and would give me her little son Adel to keep for ever. There was much laughter from all balconies and as Adel's grin spread each side of the orange he was eating the juice ran stickily down his emerald green jersey.

Selim took me into Cairo on the Metro. This is actually a tramway, and by far the most peaceful form of public transport. As it ran through the suburbs I was actually able to look out of the windows. I saw a woman walking with a gas cylinder balanced on her head. With her foot she rolled a second cylinder and negotiated the traffic of a busy main road.

'Everyone welcome you, with their eyes,' Selim assured me, to explain the curious looks I was getting. In my jacket, trousers and shirt I stood out a mile from the travelling public, and might just as well have had a green face and antennae. They were looks of kindly interest, however, not of hostility.

I was constantly delighted by the way people helped each other. An old old granny sat on the floor of the tram, and as soon as she needed to get off, strong arms were ready to help her up. A beggar made his way through the tram and many hands flew to pockets to give just a little.

'We like to help each other,' said Selim. People pick up dropped things for each other readily, hold each others' bags or babies in a relaxed and friendly way.

We went to Al Azhar Mosque, but for some reason it was not open to the public, so we couldn't go in. Outside each door of a mosque is a clean marble area surrounded by a low wall. You sit on the wall to take your shoes off, and then step on to the cool marble to go in. Attendants look after your shoes for you at the door until you come out. We tried both entrances, but were told we could not go in today. All sorts of terrible trashy souvenirs and junk were being sold from stalls outside and also in the street bazaar nearby. Against the wall of the mosque several bedraggled old men slumped in the sun. As we watched some other men, scarcely better dressed, handed bowls of flavoured rice and 'macarona' to them, which they accepted without a word.

'This food from government,' explained Selim.

We walked miles looking at shops and stalls. Some of Selim's less well prepared sentences were a bit problematical.

'Weeding closes,' he said, pointing to white bridal dresses. 'Medicine planets' (herbalist), 'Deet house' as we passed the massed tombs of the City of the Dead. The one that had me completely baffled he had two goes at:

'We have tea after mushroom.'

'?'

'After misou,' he confirmed, striding on.

Hot, dry and thirsty I panted after him to what turned out to be the Egyptian Mushroom/Misou where the Treasures of Tutenkhamoun are exhibited. Very much like the British Mushroom really, but tattier. The gold and jewels from the tombs were amazing both in quality of preservation and quantity. Many of the hieroglyphics looked as if they had been cut or painted only yesterday. This I found the most moving—the feeling of contact with a writing hand of so long ago.

The best jewels were in a side room with a notice saying:

'Only 25 people at a time in this room. Do not lean on the cases or touch the exhibits.'

Inside were about a hundred people, and a warden standing on a chair constantly clapping his hands shouting to move them round and reminding them of the notice:

'Donztushleen! G'round!'

After about an hour I could absorb no more, nor could Selim. He had never been to the museum before, and was surprised by, and proud of, what he saw.

'Peoples from all the worléd come to Egypt to see this,' he said thoughtfully.

We took a bus to the station and then the train back home. Unfortunately we hit the rush hour. The first train was impossibly crowded and a huge number of boys, a soldier and an old man rode on the engine. I took a picture of them and the boys were thrilled.

'Me? Me?' they shouted and smiled big wide Egyptian smiles as the train groaned out. A round granny in a long black dress raced along the platform at the last minute and a forest of arms hauled her aboard and somehow stuffed her in.

We got seats in the next train, but so many people piled in after us that they were hanging out of the open doors. One lad had a good idea. He hoisted the huge laundry basket that he was carrying on to the overhead hand-rails and then climbed up and sat on it. One stop before home we had to start pushing through towards the door—it was nearly impossible, but I received a good lesson in rush-hour manipulation from a young girl who did a rapid sinuous lateral sort of belly dance and rippled through the crowd. Somehow we managed to get off, but I felt afterwards that I would rather have ridden the engine with the boys.

I was invited to a meal with the downstairs Sawys. Piquant smells wafted up the stairs while I waited to be summoned. Little Asmaq pattered up the stairs and went to see what her aunt was doing. I could hear Zeinab murmuring her prayers in the bedroom.

'Tayyib,' (Good) whispered Asmaq, nodding approvingly, and went downstairs again. Rarely did more than twenty minutes go by in the flat before there was the sound of feet on the stairs and a little knock. It would be someone coming for a chat, to borrow something, to give something or sometimes just to sit.

At last Hussein came to get me. Downstairs a small candle, flickering on the table, obscured the chipped concrete walls and made the room look romantic. Actually the candle was lit because there was a power cut (they seem to happen daily) and eventually Hussein thought of taking down the bit of cardboard which blocked their one small window so that we could see a little better.

It was a wonderful meal: tasty lamb casserole, rice, roast chicken, salad, hot green peppers, bread, peas, carrots.

'Eat, Eat!' commanded Uncle Yusef, a dominating figure in his long yellow gallabiya and Omar Sharif face. His eyes shone with mock ferocity in the candle-light every time I dared to put my fork down for a short rest. It was easy to eat plenty for it was so delicious. Both Yusef and Aneesa had cooked it together, which was unusual.

Yusef knew quite a few words of English and growing more courageous as the meal went on, talked non-stop. As he gesticulated I noticed that he, like Hussein and Abdul, grew the fingernail on his little finger very long, and it was obviously a very useful and handy tool.

'My wife, she Fat!' Usef announced, loudly. 'She Very Fat. She like a . . . a . . .'

I leaned across and gently covered his mouth with his scarf, saying 'No, no! Mish kwayyis! (not kind!)'. The children leaned forward, waiting to see what their father would do. After a brief pause he roared with laughter, and they all sat back and breathed again. I was a category apart: being a woman in Egypt is a submissive role, but being a foreign woman puts one nicely outside the rules of the game. 'You can do what you like here,' Hussein told me later.

Yasmin, the prettiest of this beautiful family, kept expressing her pleasure at my visit. She sat close to me, holding my arm whenever she could, and eventually gave me a photo of herself and also a picture of Nefertiti as a present. It is strange, but in nearly every photograph I've seen of the family, they are self-conscious and all the light and character has gone out of their faces. Yasmin is ravishingly pretty, but her portrait is a great disappointment.

At about 7 o'clock I went back upstairs. Ali was home from work, but not feeling very well so he sat in a corner of the divan wrapped in a blanket. Asmaq had come upstairs with me, and we sat together at the table and drew pictures for each other. She leaned against me and her brown curls hung down over her face as she earnestly tried to draw a recognisable rabbit.

'Araanib.'

'Rabbit.'

'Rab-beet?'

'Rabbit. Now, look—carrot.'

'Gazar!'

As we sat there I wondered. She is eight years old, and in Egypt this is the age when girls are circumcised. The tradition is gradually dying out and I hoped fervently that it was not practised in this family, but at no time could I bring myself to ask.

Suddenly there was a knock at the door. Asmaq opened it and gave a squeak of delight—it was Omar. He is Sara's youngest brother, whom I hadn't met as he had been away in Alexandria. He was twenty-four, had woolly African hair and an impossibly wide smile. He put down his bags, whirled Asmaq into the air and then shook my hand. Asmaq danced round him, and then ran to fetch Zeinab.

It was a merry party that night. Omar seemed to understand more English than the rest of the family, but didn't speak it very well. He appreciated it when I teased his elder brother about his lordly behaviour, for Omar is more western in his outlook.

'You are like a king!' I said to Ali, as he gravely gave his orders after dinner. 'You sit here and everyone brings you food, and then clears it away for you.'

'I help *sometimes*,' he said, pained.

'When?'

'When nobody in house!' he had the grace to laugh at himself.

'See, I help,' he said later, pouring tea for us. He then ordered his younger brother to fetch another teaspoon.

'Tell me,' he continued, 'why does English man stir tea from left to right?'

I muttered something like 'Does he? He writes from left to right, I don't know, I hadn't noticed. . .'

'To mix sugar!' said Ali and rolled about on the divan with delight at having scored a point.

That night Omar did a solo dance lasting for half an hour. The two halves of his body I swear are not attached to each other in any way. His legs are made of flexible rubber, his feet don't touch the floor and his arms and hands can tell a whole story. It was wonderful to watch him, and the whole performance had to be 'sotto voce' as Ali had gone to bed early in the next room, so all our giggles were intensified by being stifled. Zeinab kept trying to stop him, but he'd shimmy up to her and with a neat flick of the hips, would bonk her on the bottom, making her laugh until she had to mop her eyes with her headcloth. Hussein played up to his belly-dancing by licking a pound note and sticking it to Omar's forehead. He wiggled around keeping it there, and then coyly tucked it into his bosom—the rhythm never stopping for a moment. At midnight he finally wound down, gleaming and streaming with sweat, and we crept off to bed. It was going to be difficult to leave this family.

CHAPTER 5

This morning Omar and Hussein spent a lot of time trying to tell me something. They kept pointing to the newspaper and saying 'Ahram! We go Ahram!' The name of the main Cairo newspaper is 'Al Ahram', but I couldn't understand what they meant until eventually they pointed to the little illustration—an 'Ahram' is a Pyramid.

As I was leaving for Fayoum the next day I thought it would be a good idea to wash all my clothes before we went out, so I gathered them all together.

'Give,' said Amal, holding out her arms.

'No, I'll do them,' I insisted. Amal had already washed a few things for me and I felt bad enough about that. Zeinab then offered to do them, but I wouldn't give in, so they both escorted me to the bathroom. In a corner was a tiny red plastic stool about four inches high. I was commanded to squat down on this. Then they put a large bowl on the floor in front of me, poured in hot water and gave me a packet of grey washing powder. Standing back in the passageway by the door, they folded their arms and settled down to watch. Keeping as calm as possible I consulted my confused memory. What on earth do I do at home? Oh yes, bung it all in the machine and switch on. I took a bright orange sock, which used to be pale blue before the sand got at it, sprinkled a little grey powder on it and began to rub. Nothing happened. I looked up and saw Zeinab and Amal holding on to each other and shaking silently. It was time to give in. As I went down the stairs with Omar and Hussein the laughter in the bathroom was still audible.

Omar decided that we would go to the Pyramids in style and use a taxi. Not the grand taxis used by tourists, but the 'people's taxi'. They are much cheaper and the method of using this service is well worth learning. You stand in the middle of the road and allow the traffic to pour round you. When you spot a taxi you wait until it's near enough then bawl the name of your destination in at the open window. If the driver feels like going in that direction, or else already has a passenger going somewhere near, he will stop and take you on board. Otherwise you continue to bawl into every passing taxi until you achieve success. When you arrive at your destination, you give the driver an amount which you feel is appropriate for the fare. If this is done with courtesy and confidence it is generally acceptable. The taxis do have meters in them, but few of them seem to work.

At the third or fourth attempt we managed to get a taxi to stop. There was already one passenger in the back, so Hussein and I squeezed in alongside him, and Omar got in the front. The driver had his small son with him, his nose streaming and sticky. Omar took him on his knee and chatted happily to him all the way.

The last stretch of the road to Giza is a smart dual carriageway, and down the centre is a neatly clipped hedge with topiary pyramids every few hundred yards. Omar paid the driver satisfactorily and we began to walk up towards the Pyramids at the edge of the desert which comes to an abrupt stop at the side of the road.

Men with horses and camels came crowding after us shouting, offering rides, but the boys politely rejected their services and we continued to walk. We got as far as the Great Pyramid and started to climb it, but one camel driver had followed us and was shouting angrily, so Omar went down to speak to him. The driver was convinced that the boys had hired themselves out to me (illegally) as guides. I went down and tried to explain that they were my friends, but he would not listen and went off to report us to a Tourist Policeman. We were then ordered to go to the Director of Tourist Police in an office nearby and explain ourselves. Fortunately he was a reasonable man and, after looking at my passport and asking a few questions, he gave us a written permit and let us go. The boys were so patient and polite that it made my blood boil to think how they were being treated by these loud-mouthed salesmen, but I hadn't the words to express it. Perhaps it was just as well.

Back we went and had a lovely time playing with the Great Pyramid. The stone blocks are cool and as smooth as silk. We climbed about on it (strictly forbidden, but everyone does), Omar daring us to go higher and higher. Eventually we sat down in a convenient niche and, after a brief clapping and rhythm session we dropped off to sleep in the sun.

The boys insisted that I should ride a camel, but we didn't like the look of any of the drivers much. Then we noticed, far off on a hillock standing alone, an old old camel driver all in white, mounted on a camel with coloured tassels hanging on her harness. He looked like an illustration from the Bible. We hailed him and he gladly offered us a ride for a very reasonable price. He told us that the camel was called Gazelle, and he was very fond of her. I sat in front and the boys took turns to ride behind, Omar singing all the way of course. We rode round the second-sized Pyramid and then down to see the Sphynx (called 'Abu el Hool' by the Egyptians). Approached from behind it looks rather a mess, but as we came round and began to see the profile we were all moved by her wonderful serenity. (I'm sure it's a *her*). Even the boys fell silent for a moment. It is incredible how the serenity shows through although the face is so badly battered by the Turks' target-practice. At the end of the ride our dear old camel driver demanded double the price. Omar was firm however and offered him the agreed amount or nothing. He took it, grumbling, and I slipped him an extra ten piastres for his cheek.

'These people all "klifti" ', said Omar, waving a disparaging arm.The trouble is that these 'klifti' people are the only Egyptians that most tourists meet, so it is no wonder that they get the wrong idea about Egyptians.

On the way home the usual uproar of hooting cars had taken on a new rhythm: xx xxx xx xxx. There had been an important football match and the winning supporters were celebrating. The two big teams in Egypt are 'Ahli' and 'Zamalek'. Everybody supports one or the other, and there was much excitement in the family when we watched the match on television that night. There were also extracts from matches in the Africa Cup, and watching seas of brown faces shouting 'Goal! Goal!' from all parts of Africa it seemed that British influence was not quite dead.

Later on we watched the ballet 'Pineapple Poll'. Sullivan's essentially English music lay rather incongruously between a programme of traditional Arabic music, sung by Egypt's most popular singer who was a 70 year old Lebanese woman, and the nightly intoned readings from the Koran.

Amal finished ironing my clothes, and the electric iron, made in Japan, was carefully put back into its cardboard box. The blanket, which she used on the table instead of an ironing board, was folded and put away.

This was my last night with the family, the next day I would be an independent traveller. So far, apart from my telephone call home, 10 piastres to a beggar and 10 piastres to the camel driver, I had not been allowed to pay for anything. Not only did the boys always insist on paying, but I suspected that they were taking time off work and school to take me around, and I felt very guilty. It was certainly time to go.

At about 10 o'clock Hussein came upstairs to say goodnight and pressed something into my hand. When I looked, I saw a ticket—a ticket to Fayoum for the next morning. He had been out to buy it for me, and wouldn't let me pay. As I fumbled for words which were sufficiently emphatic, he fingered his little moustache and smiled contentedly.

16

CHAPTER 6

The road across the desert stretched out ahead, a straight khaki stripe between banks of khaki grit. It wasn't as deserted as I had expected as there were pylons and army camps and huts scattered about. Every few miles a soldier at a checkpoint made notes on the passing traffic. I was on the way to Fayoum, a town in the middle of an oasis 64 miles south-west of Cairo. This oasis is the most fertile farming area in Egypt, where most of the vegetables for Cairo are grown. My plan was to stay in the town and explore the oasis by whatever means were available. On the western edge of the oasis was Lake Kharoun which I also wanted to see.

Omar had come with me to Rameses station that morning, and gone through all the necessary questioning to find the right bus in the muddy jumble of the bus depôt behind the station. Nobody seemed to be quite sure where or when anything was going, but at last I was installed in the front seat of a coach and the girl next to me was instructed to look after me.

Before we left, a boy with a tray of sweets and chewing-gum had leapt on and dropped a packet in each passenger's lap. As he came back along the coach he collected either the money for it, or the unwanted packet. Before I had got this routine worked out the girl next to me had paid for my packet, and given me a happy smile.

After we had been going about half an hour, an old man came forward and tapped the coach driver urgently on the shoulder. The coach stopped, and the old fellow climbed down the steps, went a few paces away in the sand and crouched down, spreading his robe round him. A few moments later, looking much happier, he climbed back on board, and we were off again.

At last a green smudge appeared on the horizon, which focused itself into palm trees, and soon we were passing through farm land where, although it was winter, the crops were growing abundantly. We arrived in the town and were dropped off beside a stagnant looking canal. I shouldered my rucksack and, feeling very conspicuous, walked along to find a hotel of some sort. Fayoum seemed more like a village than a town. The main street had shops and stalls and there were some large buildings and factories on the outskirts. Orange sellers squatted by the canal, their dusty fruit piled in pyramids. The side streets leading off the main street were mostly unmade and contained small apartment blocks. No sign of any hotels.

As I went along people called out

'Hello!'

'What's your name?'

'How old are you?'

'Can I be of some service to you?'

It was quite difficult to cope with at first, but a cheerful smile, a wave and 'Leeh, shokran' (no, thank you) was sufficient to send them off satisfied. At a newspaper stall by the station I asked:

'Lukanda hinna?' (Hotel here?) The young man grinned and pointed to a building behind me. It had a murky entrance rather like a disused garage, and on the wall at the front the word 'hotel' was painted in crooked red lettering. I didn't go in, but wandered off again.

In the centre of the town are some famous waterwheels. They are very ancient and of an unusual design. The water pours from holes round the side of the wheels, making a silvery kaleidoscope of spray. The sound and sight of pouring water with the sunlight shining through it was magnetic, and a small crowd was always there watching them. Alongside was a tea-garden and to give myself time to think I sat down to enjoy the splashing water and drink tea.

The only piece of information that the Thomas Cook office had let slip when I questioned them, was the name of a hotel on Lake Kharoun. It seemed a good idea to try to get there, as there seemed to be nowhere to stay in the town. The waiter directed me to some buses standing in a muddy lane.

'Long way. Take bus.'

Which bus? I found someone who looked like a driver leaning against a tree smoking and tried out my few words on him. He was delighted to help and escorted me down the lane to the spot where the Kharoun bus would come in. We stood and talked, managing pretty well considering our respective limitations, and I was very glad that I had learned my few words and had a good vocabulary book in my pocket. A battered bus drew up with green paint sloshed across the tops of the windows to keep the sun out. My friend leapt on, pushing everyone else aside, and ushered me into the front seat. He gave the driver the name of the hotel I had heard about, and although there was a tremendously energetic exchange of words about this, everything appeared to be settled. He was much too genuinely friendly to tip, so I swung him a hefty Egyptian handshake (the men whack their right hands together and then shake) which pleased him no end, coming from a foreign lady.

Sharing my seat were two very squashed schoolgirls in long dark brown gallabiyas and white headcloths, looking like miniature nuns. Everything I did fascinated them, particularly writing in my notebook from left to right. They nudged each other and smiled shyly at me. One girl took out 'Living English—Book I' from her school bag and gently pushed it into my hands. I read a page to them and they were thrilled, although I had to shout through the noise of the rattletrap bus, the continuous excitable chatter of the passengers and the shower of feathers from two live hens held upside down by a soldier standing just beside us.

We passed through villages of increasing primitiveness, past farmlands gleaming green shaded by groves of palm trees. Water buffalo and goats grazed peacefully and barefoot children in rags paddled in the mud-and-water irrigation channels. Fellaheen rode by on donkeys, swinging their legs with sandals balanced on their upturned toes. Then we ran out of tarmac road.

All the passengers had got off by now except a friend of the driver who swapped places with him while the bus was going and had a turn at driving. He had dreadful trouble with the gear lever, which was sometimes a two-handed job, and the bus bounced and clattered over the potholed track. On and on, through the flat, flat farmland. I was alternately paralysed with nervousness and fascinated by the countryside. At this point my notebook reads:

'What the hell am I doing here? *Enormous* tomatoes.'

I could sense that the lake was near as the air was suddenly cooler. The men kept up a constant vigorous high-spirited backchat all the way to the last village, which was the most primitive of all. There were mud brick huts with wonky chimneys and all manner of stuff on the flat roofs, torn awnings of filthy sacking, donkeys, carts, mud and rubbish everywhere and a great colourful crowd blocking the roadway, all busy doing nothing in particular. I had kept preparing myself for the worst as far as this 'hotel' was concerned, but began to feel perhaps I hadn't done it thoroughly enough.

Suddenly the bus swung round the corner, narrowly missing an old granny sitting in the dust, and there was the lake. The water was dark, and the sandhills on the far side shone like heaps of ripe wheat in the evening sunshine. Another mile or two along the shore and then suddenly:

'Here you are—welcome—have a happy time.'

I staggered out, rather numb after 1½ hours of jolting, and walked straight into the foyer of a most sumptuous hotel. Heavy oak panelling, carved furniture, hanging brass bowls of trailing plants, fat white twisty pillars, many many-branched lights, soft carpet, soft music. English spoken well. I groaned—this was not what I had come to see.

'Yes, madam, of course. How much? £45 for bed. No, breakfast is extra.'

Feeling depressed, and terribly conspicuous in my dusty trousers and crumpled jacket I was shown to an immense bedroom with a triple bed. Adjoining it was a bathroom like a marble temple.

It seemed sensible, as there was no escape possible because night falls at 5 o'clock, to make the best of it and so I ran the bath. Water welled up through the floor and began to flood the whole room. I rang for the housekeeper who transferred me to another room, equally grand. She hoovered round me while I sat and sulked. Although the hotel was new there was a line of damp rotting through the walls. This bathroom had no plug to the bath, so I had to use an upturned tooth mug held in place with my foot. During the evening the fire alarm went off periodically, but on looking out of my door I saw a man with a screwdriver gazing anxiously about, so I knew there was no need to worry. A glass of tonic cost me 85p. The Spaghetti Bolognese was a disaster as the spaghetti was cooked without salt, and the Bolognese came out of a tin—you could taste the tin. Over a cup of tepid tea I frantically worked at my budget.

'Will you take a drink with me?' A smooth businessman in a smooth brown suit had taken the next chair.

'No, I'm sorry, I have some work to do.'

'I will meet you here at six o'clock,' he decided. 'Which room are you in?'

'I can't remember the number,' I lied smoothly, and left him looking thoughtful.

So there I was amidst unwanted luxury, at the Sahara desert end of a dead-end track 1½ hours long. As I wrote up my notes, the triple bed was witness to my solitary tears and laughter that night.

CHAPTER 7

Breakfast was a miniature omelette, two slices of plastic toast and more tepid tea. I ramed it all down, not knowing where the next meal might be coming from. My total bill when I checked out was £63.21. When I asked them to help me telephone another hotel further along the lake, which I hoped might be cheaper, they smiled politely and said that they couldn't find the number. They wouldn't take travellers' cheques or credit cards, although their smart literature said that they did.

'You can't do *anything*.'

'We are sorry,' they replied, smiling plastic smiles.

'Me too,' I said, and stumped out.

Outside were rows of buses and hundreds of school children. Friday is a holiday in Egypt when many people go on excursions. These children had come to row about in boats and enjoy the colourful delights of the little pier by the hotel. I looked around for the public service bus like the one which brought me the previous night, but couldn't really tell one from another, so I stood waiting for another helpful-looking bus driver to come into view.

Some smart teenage boys in navy blazers were looking hard at me. They moved closer and debated together, staring even harder. Eventually one came forward and said politely.

'Please, one picture?' gesturing with his camera. I suddenly realised that I was a curiosity; one of those engaging, eccentric characters that we English go abroad to photograph and chuckle over when we get home.

'O.K.' I said, resignedly. Immediately they all rushed forward and grouped themselves picturesquely, two with their arms round me. I couldn't help laughing. Another picture, then another, then I shooed them off. 'Bass, bass!' It was only after they had gone that I noticed my trouser zip was undone.

Behind me hundreds of small boys were all trying to get into a single-decker coach at once. The noise was incredible and the camel/eye-of-needle effect was intensified by the fact that most of them had bought highly coloured plastic umbrellas, palm-leaf baskets or shell necklaces from the pier. I took a photo of their mad scrambling which amused them. One of their teachers came over and asked my nationality. As soon as I said 'English' his face lit up with a smile.

'I English teacher with this primary school from Minia,' he said, waving an arm towards the tangle of limbs behind him. 'Can I help you?'

I told him I wanted to take the service bus back to Fayoum.

'There is no public bus—only excurison buses.'

I insisted that there must be one, because I had arrived on it the previous night. He went off to check, but no, there wasn't one. That meant that yesterday's bus had made a special trip just to deliver me, and all for 20p. I told him about the cost of the hotel and that I needed to get back to Cairo to visit a bank before I could continue my travels.

'No problem,' he beamed. 'You come with us.' The school party was going on a tour which would end up at Fayoum town, where I could catch the bus to Cairo.

'How much will it cost?' I asked, a bit anxiously, as my cash was getting low.

'Nothing, nothing,' he insisted. He turned to the scrum behind us, skilfully pushed a way through, and put me into the seat of honour at the front. I watched amazed as the boys were somehow counted in, 120 of them. The English teacher had three on his lap, so I relieved him of one—an enchanting little boy with big dark eyes.

The roll was called, or rather bellowed through the microphone by one of the other teachers:

'Muhammed Hassan, Ali Muhammed, Ahmed Ali Hassan, Selim Muhammed, Hassan Ali . . .'

We bounced and rolled as the shouting, whistling, singing, drumming cargo was driven over the rough road between the green fields and blue-green palm groves. Grazing water buffalo, their hides of gunmetal sheen, didn't bother to look up, nor did the goats. Donkey carts padded by along the road, and our driver hooted at every one, which added to the din. There was a lull in the chatter as we passed a solemn crowd of fellaheen all in clean, well-pressed robes, carrying a coffin draped with a red and gold carpet. The men chanted softly as they walked. An old man led his camel which was so loaded with green fodder that only its neck and splayed bony legs showed. Although the country folk were poor, nobody seemed to be starving and the cultivated land looked well tended and fruitful.

Over the din and the hooting, Emad, the English teacher, questioned me about myself: my name, age and profession, my family.

'Where is your husband?'

I shouted back the answers and my personal details were then bawled down the bus in Arabic, causing tremendous merriment.

'You want food?'

'Not yet, thanks.'

But you can't stop Egyptians from feeding you. A massive grey bread roll, filled with cold sliced potatoes, was thrust into my hand. I held it for a long time and finally packed it with ceremonial care and gratitude into my rucksack.

'For later. Thank you.'

We had about an hour at Selin Springs, a mineral spring surrounded by a pleasure park. Sitting in cane chairs under the shade of the dusty trees, Emad and I drank tea and he studied my English map of Egypt with close concentration. He asked me a great deal about the English language, some of the questions I found incredibly difficult to answer. He was particularly fascinated by idioms and proverbs.

'You know these?' he asked. ' "Every dog is a lion at home." "If you deal with a fox, think of his tricks." "Too much bed makes a dull head." "The fool says I can't but the wise man says I'll try." "Those who live in glass-houses must throw them with stones . . ." '

I confessed to knowing only—um—one of those. Perhaps the others were American-English ones.

'When you in England, can you send me book?'

'Yes, of course. What book?'

'Book about teaching English. I cannot get such a book in Egypt.'

I agreed, remembering an excellent bookshop back home, with a section of English for Foreigners. It was my turn to say 'No problem! You gave me transport—I will send you books.'

A solemn, middle-aged looking boy of twelve in a three-piece blue serge suit glided up to us, and with solemn gesture presented us with a bottle of fizzy orange to drink. Then the other boys, bored with looking at the mineral spring, began to drift back. A small group of them sang some songs for me.

The previous day Fayoum town had looked like a large market village, but when I returned there, after the bus journey through tiny primitive villages, it looked like a metropolis. The teachers escorted me to the

Cairo bus, shoved through the scrum of farmers, soldiers and muscular old ladies and got me a front seat.

'Do not forget me,' begged Emad as he fought his way off.

The bus was hot and crowded. In spite of this, tattered energetic individuals leapt on and pushed through the tightly packed bodies to sell Pepsi-Cola, sweets, chewing-gum, newspapers, combs and laces. When they had negotiated the whole length of the bus they would leap off while it was still moving, never dropping anything. I admired their energy and the way they never minded if you refused their goods.

Shopping bags and parcels were stuffed tightly round my legs, and a man in a puce satin jacket and green woolly hat leaned heavily on my left shoulder all the way to Cairo. Two of the muscular farm ladies sat cross-legged on the next seat, hunched like witches, their dusty bare toes poking out from under their black dresses. Soldiers in badly mended uniforms hung from the luggage rack. There was the usual cacophony of shouting, laughing and the driver hooting at every other vehicle we met on the desert road. Then at last the pyramids loomed up ahead, golden in the sunset. Home at last. (That last couple of sentences—how strange. Less than a week before I could not have written them.)

The bus stopped at Giza by a wall which smelled strongly of—well, there's nowhere to stop on the desert road. The camel drivers were bringing their camels down from the pyramids, the gaudy tassels on the harness muted by the quickly darkening sky. Mini-buses were lined up and, not feeling like a scrum on another public bus, I found one whose driver was shouting 'Rameses, Rameses.'

'Bikaam Midaan Rameses?'

'50 piastres madaam. I take care of you. Please sit here in front seat. Anything you want to know, informations about Cairo, ask me.'

A young boy of about eighteen sat next to me and the pressure of his leg against mine increased as the journey progressed. Feeling sorry that this was the best he could do in the way of sexual excitement, given the Muslim customs, I groped for the words with which to say 'Now then, my boy, I'm old enough to be your mother,' but hadn't quite got it all together by the time we arrived.

Rameses Square in the dark. The walkway high above the grinding traffic was dimly lit. Hurrying robed figures poured in all directions. Dark turbaned faces, lit by the flicker of flames from coffee and sweetcorn roasting, punctuated the darkness. The old lady with the enormous baskets full of tiny lemons was in her usual place by the station entrance, and the fruit seemed luminous. A few days before I had been confused by it all, but now it felt like home.

I took the train to the suburb where the Sawy family lived and knocked apologetically at the door. I needed to beg a bed for one more night as the banks are closed on Fridays. The mother and father were there alone and at first I took their slight hesitation for displeasure, but later noticed that the divans were now covered with dull, everyday covers, and the flat was not quite so immaculate as before.

I had to explain my whole story in Arabic as they knew no English at all.

'Fayoum. No hotel. Lake Kharoun—hotel—£45—bed only!'

Expressions of horror and incredulity crossed their faces. I struggled on.

'Money finish. Today banks closed—Friday. Tomorrow bank, then Luxor. Tonight, please, one bed?'

I have always maintained that grammar is unnecessary, mainly because I find it difficult to learn. They understood at once and were sympathetic and welcoming, and I was given my old room.

Gradually the family returned and were told the story of my adventure. To celebrate my return we ate hugely. The word 'Eat!' with its imperative exclamation mark is surely the most used word in Egypt.

Then Yasmin from downstairs came up and invited us to drink tea and see her sister Nargis, who was taken ill the day I left, and has since had her appendix out. Nargis was withdrawn and silent, propped up on a divan with lumpy cushions. Aneesa, her mother, made vague sympathetic moaning noises, but didn't do much to comfort her. Yasmin was wonderful with Nargis, feeding her and gently helping her when she wanted to move. When I arrived there was much handshaking and many welcoming kisses and exclamations at my early return. I gave Nargis a specially warm cuddle to try to convey everything I wanted to say without words. She smiled her strange, silent smile and later whispered to Yasmin to tell me how pleased she was that I had come. Another little sister, Neget, is shy too, but that night for the first time she came and sat close, leaning against me. What a load of loving.

'The Magnificent Seven' kept us all up late sitting round on the divans cuddled up under blankets. Then, as the downstairs Sawys' cats had their final fight on the stairs, I retired to my room to sleep.

CHAPTER 8

The next morning Omar and I set out to find Barclays Bank. The bus was incredibly crowded as ever, but Omar and I made a big joke of it all, and held on to each other giggling like schoolgirls. As soon as the bus conductor learned that I was English I was invited to occupy the free space beside his seat, and I perched on a high bar over the wheel-arch feeling conspicuous. More unseemly giggling.

Barclays was closed as it was Saturday, and in England banks close on Saturdays. All the other banks in Cairo were open of course.

'We go home?' said Omar, with the usual Egyptian acceptance of defeat.

'Nonsense! Follow me,' I cried, and led him, blinking nervously, into Shepheards Hotel. I greeted the fleet of blue and gold sultans in the foyer with cheerful confidence, and swanned into the hotel bank. The transaction was brief, efficient and at a good rate of exchange. Only later did I realise, with feelings of guilt, that Omar had watched me casually handling the equivalent of, for him, six months' wages.

Julian, a friend in England, had given me the telephone number of an Egyptian in Luxor who would help me to find somewhere to stay. I needed to 'phone him, but didn't fancy the long queues at the station telephone office. The switchboard at Shepheards Hotel was out of order, so, high on success, we bounced into the imposing Cleopatra Hotel, where the switchboard operator efficiently connected me with Taha in Luxor.

'Hello. This is June. I'm a friend of Julian, in England.'

'Oh yes. Good. You come to Luxor?'

'Yes, on the mid-day train.'

'Fine. O.K. No problem. I meet you.'

Omar and I walked through the streets chewing nuts, occasionally stopping at stalls to drink freshly crushed orange, guava or sugar cane juice, ice cold and delicious.

Going through traffic with Omar was like dancing. Sometimes his hand held my elbow with a firm grip, sometimes he took me by the hand,

and always his subtle rhythmic movements rippled us safely through. Every now and then he turned and beamed.

'You O.K.?'

'Yes.'

'Me O.K. too. You happy, me happy.'

The whole city seems to have a rhythm and tempo of its own. At one point we were negotiating the incredibly complicated cross-flow of traffic in Tahrir Square. In addition to his dancing in and out of the moving cars, Omar wanted to light a cigarette. Having no matches, he swung alongside an old grandpa, took his cigarette, lit his own from it and giving it back with courteous thanks, continued without breaking the rhythm for a moment.

'No problem!' he grinned, and the grandpa didn't seem to mind either.

Two grey-faced Australians at the station obviously hadn't got the feel of it yet. 'Suppose they'll want our whole flamin' life story before we get our ticket—Jesus!'

Of course they want your life story—can't you see why? And if they do tend to begin 'What's your name? How old are you?' it is only because that was in chapter one of their English text book at school.

We were a bit late for the train, but Omar, by some unseemly scrambling over the tracks (quicker than the subway) dragged me to the right platform and got me on just in time.

As the train rolled south I suddenly felt lonely, so wrote a long and wobbly letter to my children.

Dear Rachel and Daniel,

'Here I am alone on a train in the middle of Africa'. That's a slight exaggeration, but try saying that to yourself and believing it. It gives you a funny feeling.

I left Cairo at noon, and expect to arrive in Luxor at midnight. Cairo is the modern capital of Egypt as you know, but Luxor was the capital in the time of the Pharoahs and is thick with ruined temples and palaces.

Julian's friend Taha said he would meet me when I arrive. I hope he doesn't forget. Midnight is a bit late to have no bed to go to, but Egypt is such a relaxed, happy-go-lucky country that it is quite difficult to get anxious.

I really wanted to get the 8 a.m. train so that I would see the whole Nile valley in daylight, but that wasn't possible. Darkness falls quickly here, between 5 and 6 p.m. The haze of sand hanging over the western Sahara makes some marvellous sunsets, all tomato-ketchup and molten gold.

Coming south out of Cairo the suburbs and factories straggled on and on. Suburbs not like Finchley or Wimbledon, but crazy, bare-brick, flat-roofed higgledy-piggledy heaps of assorted dwellings with piles of stuff on the roofs: drying stalks, sacks, pots, and even ducks, hens and geese.

People seem to live in the lower rooms of a building before the top ones are complete. Either that, or else perhaps when the house is full they just start sticking more rooms on top. Not sure which. Everywhere seems like a building site with litter, rubble, bricks, planks, iron rods and of course goats, water buffaloes and children having a great time in what must be one of the biggest, dustiest adventure playgrounds in the world. Most of the children I saw were barefoot, but look well-fed and happy. So do the animals, you'll be pleased to hear. I've only seen one really thin horse. Egyptians seem to have a good relationship with their animals. I've seen no cruelty such as you hear about in many eastern countries.

Have you ever seen a water buffalo, by the way? It is rather like a badly designed cow with an invisible heavy weight on its head. Its shiny grey hide hangs like a Bedouin tent on its bony frame. If a camel is 'a horse designed by a committee' I don't know how the water buffalo got put together.

One of the loveliest sights I've seen today was a girl of about ten, slim and graceful, riding a slender grey donkey. They moved together in perfect harmony and how she guided it I don't know, but it went just where she wanted, while she leaned back enjoying the sun.

When the train got away from the city into proper countryside the vegetation grew thicker. The palms were taller and the crops further on, although it is mid-winter. We passed many small villages, much like even sandier, muddier versions of the Cairo suburbs. Each had its own small mosque, often with a dome and a crescent where you'd expect a cross to be on a church. There were burial plots outside each village, each with a little domed temple. Some graves were just mounds, and others had a stone at the head and foot. Graceful plumed reeds wave in the irrigation channels which run alongside the railway track.

Over by the Nile in the distance are the tall chimneys of brick factories, but the view from the train is mostly of fields. The rectangles of different crops are divided from each other by either a shallow ridge or a ditch. In some of the groves of palm trees there are shelters for animals, necessary in the hot summer. Today the animals stood about in the sun munching some bright green leafy crop which looks like clover and grows everywhere. Most of the farming seems to be done by hand, with tools much like those pictured in the temples 3,000 years ago. I've only seen one tractor so far today. Beyond the fields runs the Nile, out of sight most of the time, and beyond that, in sharp contrast to the bright green, are the pale gold cliffs of the Eastern Desert.

One useful thing I have learned from the Egyptians is Just Sitting. They do it a lot, and it is a useful art. Every negotiation takes at least four times longer than it would in England, so you Just Sit, often either on your haunches or on the ground. At the flat in Cairo the popular alternative to television is Just Sitting on the balcony, watching the street.

By the way, I saw 'Pineapple Poll' on television yesterday. It was advertised in the Cairo English newspaper as 'The Pineapple Fruit'. How people connected the title with all those leaping sailors I can't imagine. T.V. is quite good here. It was fun to see shots of England yesterday with people shovelling snow trying to get their cars out of drifts. There are programmes about the development of Egypt, decent English and American films, lots *of Arab music and dancing, Window on the World, Candid Camera, readings from the Koran. It must have a tremendous impact on people in the remote villages.*

We've just stopped at Sohag station. Dark turbaned faces keep peering in at me and knocking on the windows, just like people do in zoos. I just waved to a little boy on the platform whose smile flashed in the dark like a whole piano keyboard.

I'll write again from Luxor. I feel a long way from you, my dears, but sitting writing this is almost like talking to you, which helps.

Give Daddy a hug from me.

love, Mum.

The train ground on slowly. At 6 o'clock a perfect moon hung over the Eastern Desert. A meal was served on a tray comprising several little containers covered with plastic film. In them were tender slices of beef, flavoured rice, green peppers stuffed with lentils, vegetables in sauce, yogurt with bits of olive in and a piece of sweet cake. Money for this, and a succession of glasses of tea, was collected late in the evening by a smiling waiter who asked me what I'd had. I paid up and thanked him for his excellent service.

'What's that word for "thank you?" ' asked one of the American students sitting opposite. I was amazed that they could have travelled for a week in the country without bothering to find out. They were totally self-absorbed and didn't bother to look out of the window, but either slept, or whined to each other about the shortcomings of the country or their internal disorders. I had reason to be grateful to them, however, as they showed me a guide-book printed in the USA for students which gives details of low budget hotels in Egypt—just what I had been looking for.

There were no late-night drunks on the train, as Egypt is technically a 'dry' country. The train went more and more slowly. The lights were dimmed at 12.20 a.m. and we were only just leaving Qena. I thought of poor Taha waiting on Luxor station. Someone once said 'If you want people to like you, let them do you a favour.' I must be very popular in Egypt. It got very cold and it wasn't until 2 a.m. that we pulled into Luxor.

I expected Taha to have given up and gone, but as I alighted a slim shivering figure, in a neat grey suit, came up and greeted me.

'It's O.K. Trains are often late. I take you to my family home now. Too late to go to a hotel.'

We drove to a narrow back street, even rougher than the one in Cairo and smelling strongly of drains. Taha took me upstairs to the flat and into his own room. It was a great contrast to the rooms at the Sawy's house, being cluttered with books, magazines, tapes, discarded socks and dirty cups and glasses—more like my son's room at home. Much to my delight Taha produced a whisky bottle and poured me a generous portion. This was the first alcohol I had seen in Egypt. I sat on the bed and he sat on the floor against the wall and went straight to the point:

'Why have you come to Egypt?'

I made some conventional remarks, but he was not fooled.

'You have come to escape—to forget?'

He was right. I had been through a difficult time, and one of the reasons for the trip was to think and to sort out priorities and values. We talked for a long time. Eventually, warmed by the whisky, and having convinced Taha that I needed to be alone, I curled up in my sleeping bag on his bed and he went to sleep with his brother.

LOTUS
HOTEL

CHAPTER 9

Luxor was hot and lazy. It was much quieter than Cairo and far less crowded. Although there were quite a few tourist groups in the grand hotels along the Corniche, they were not much in evidence as they spent most of the day being taken about in coaches and boats to see the antiquities. Nearly everyone in Luxor makes their living out of tourists, so every few yards someone offers a taxi, a horse-drawn carriage or currency exchange. Along the steep banks of the Nile graceful feluccas were moored, waiting for customers.

'Oh madaam, come at sunset. I take you sail to Banana Island. Beautiful island. My boat the best on the Nile. Only one hour. Not much money.'

'No thanks, not today.'

'Maybe tomorrow?'

'Maybe.'

'O.K. you come tomorrow.'

'Maybe.'

All the other people who didn't want to sell things wanted to try out their English.

'Hello. Welcome.'

'Welcome Madaam. Come and sit down. I want to speak for you.'

'Hello my sister!'

'Welcome to school!' This from a master shepherding his flock in through the school gates. A boy of about fifteen offered me a ride on the crossbar of his bike. Another wanted to take me home to have tea with his family. Their approach was gentle and all smiles. When I refused I smiled too, and then everyone was happy. A smile is good international currency. I wanted to say this to the two American students who were on the train, and were now in the same hotel 'doing' Luxor. They were pale, unsmiling, cynical, suspicious and mostly unimpressed by everything.

'We saw this Sound and Light thing—I didn't get much from it.'

Ali one of the felucca boys, said 'French, Germans, Americans are like snakes—only the English are good people.' I wondered what the Arabic word was for 'blarney'.

Across the river are the mountains which contain the Valley of the Kings and the Tombs of the Queens. In the morning the mountains are often invisible in the mist, by noon they have gradually changed from pale biscuit to dark brown, and by evening they turn to pure gold.

In the heat of the day I dawdled along the river bank, keeping under the trees out of the sun, and watched pictures form and reform. Two-wheeled carriages decorated with bright flowers trotted along carrying tourists. The drivers in turban and robe, resting their feet on piles of bright green clover under the driving seat, cracked their whips impressively. Placid donkeys with sleepy riders padded softly by on unshod hooves. A busy group of little goats blew delicately in the dust looked for titbits. Taxi pick-up vans passed with about ten people hanging on behind and more inside under the awning. Sometimes instead of people they carried a couple of cows or a water buffalo.

Some of the signs, in their English translations, made entertaining reading. 'Tourist Fairy this way.' 'Shady Cars.' 'Marakaibo Club—Hot Staff.' A sign fooled me for days which read:

E
M
O
C
L
E
W

until I tried reading it upwards.

Amidst all the churned up dust, to turn and look at the Nile was like taking a deep drink, and I didn't like to go far away from it. The water was dark and flowed at a certain speed, a sort of fastish walking pace, giving it an air of authority. I developed a great love for the river which I certainly didn't feel for the temples. They were big, beautiful, hot, empty and dead. I preferred the living inhabitants of Luxor and their relaxed style of life. Under one tree a man sat in a chair having his hair cut. On the footpath in front of Luxor Temple a body slept. An old man sat alone smoking a hookah. A small discussion group was assembled on some boulders by a tree. The women in their long black street dresses moved more purposefully, carrying big wicker baskets full of shopping on their heads. I was intrigued to watch some workmen on a building site. The only tools they had were long-handled shovels and large-headed hoes, and they used small two-handled baskets to carry rubble away. Two men were mixing cement: one turned the mixture over and the other pulled on a rope attached to the shovel to help take the strain, the two of them moving in perfect rhythm.

My hotel was called The Lotus Hotel, but with the usual disregard for accuracy in the placing of vowels, the key ring was stamped 'Louts Hotel'. It had four bedrooms on each floor and a bathroom which cried out for a tin of Vim. As soon as I arrived I had a good shower and washed my hair. I had been wandering around on the landing with a towel round my head when I suddenly remembered that Muslim women sometimes do this to indicate that their husbands have just made love to them. Ritual all-over washing is compulsory after intercourse. I retired discreetly to my room to dry my hair in private.

The restaurant was on the top floor of the hotel, and there was a good view of the Nile if you stood on a chair—the windows were too high. If the cook needed fresh supplies for his kitchen he leaned out of the window and yelled. When he got a response from below he hurled a basket out. The basket was attached to a table leg by a length of string which was then used to haul it up when the appropriate signal was given. Meals were basic, but tasty, consisting generally of soup followed by meat and rice or macaroni and then fruit.

I spent a very happy few days just wandering round looking, and writing in the evenings. People gradually realised that I wasn't a Tourist who wanted rides or souvenirs, and so would just call greetings or as in the case of Ali—the felucca boy, just talk.

I would usually meet Taha each morning in the gardens of one of the big hotels by the river and he would be ready to help with any advice I needed. I found it was an accepted custom to stay in a small cheap hotel and then make use of the beautiful gardens and elegant cloakrooms of the larger hotels. It was while we sat under the trees sipping tea that Taha told me his life story.

CHAPTER 10

I was born in 1952 in a small village between Luxor and the airport. Our house was quite large. Downstairs was mostly for visitors, and also had places for the animals. Upstairs was for sleeping. When I was five I was sent to the village school. There an old man taught us to read and write and to recite the Koran. There were about 14 of us. He had a stick and would beat us to keep the Koran in our minds. My father did not like this so he took me away and sent me to a school in Luxor run by Americans. This was much better, but only taught the Christian religion so at seven I moved again to the public school in Luxor where the Muslim religion is taught.

In our house lived my mother and father, my grandfather, my brother and my four sisters. In those days the villages were happy places. When we sat down to our main meal there was always some dish prepared for us as a gift from one of the neighbours. People were kind to each other and good to their families. Everybody had enough to eat. How could they want what they didn't know about? But of course this is not fair. Nowadays when people are living the faster life, some of this kindness is dying out and being forgotten. Television teases our people by showing them things they cannot have. Brothers forget their duties to their families as this false civilisation overtakes them. The poor who were happy are now discontented.

A few years after I went to the school in Luxor the government wanted land to build new canals, so we had to leave our house. They gave us some compensation. We then moved into Luxor and I continued normal education until I was 18, when I got my secondary school degree.

I then wanted to go to the Industrial College in Assiut, but my father made me go to the Commercial Faculty. I was obstinate and failed my first year exams on purpose. I wasted a whole year, but really I did not waste it for I spent a lot of time reading and it cleared my mind. I read the classical literature of Egypt, and then moved on to foreign literature: Gorky, Tolstoi, Dostoievsky, Jack London, Shakespeare and the French philosophers. At this time I also began to write. I remember that I burned my first story! When my mind began to clear, I started to question God, and lost my belief in Islam. Then I began to read about Communism: Marx, Engels and so on, although it was difficult to get translations of foreign literature as Sadat closed down all the bookshops from 1970-1980.

I never joined the Communist party—I am *myself*, and I am Egypt as I imagine it in my mind.

In 1974 the police began to watch me. I started doing social work and began a sort of youth club where boys were helped with their lessons, played games, taken to the theatre. After two months the police closed it down.

In October 1974 the new university term began. In November the police had orders to catch me and 100 other students from Assiut, a thousand from Cairo University and so on—you can imagine the size of the operation. The charge was that we organised secret Communist activities against the government. This was at the time when the country was closed to Russia and opened to the USA. Any criticism of the government indicated that you were a Communist. If you wrote that the streets were dirty you were a Communist.

I evaded the police in Assiut until January 1975, then I went home. I was tired out and slept late. The next morning the police came to the house to get me when I was still in bed.

'Can I get dressed, get money and things together?'

'No, you come now.'

'By law you need a warrant to take me—where is it?'

'What do you know of the law?'

'I know the law. Where is the warrant?'

'At the police station.'

'You be kind to me and let me get dressed and I will come to the police station with you.'

The policeman went into the kitchen to drink tea. I went to my room and dressed. Then I jumped from the third floor window and got out of Luxor on the next train to Assiut. (That night my father burned all my foreign literature.)

I rented a room in Assiut and lived there for the next few months. I disguised myself by wearing a gallabiyya and glasses and growing a moustache. The trouble was that I had no books. The end of year exams were coming soon and I didn't want to waste yet another year. I sent a message to a friend to get my books to me but he was afraid. In the end I managed to borrow some.

In order to graduate I had to pass six out of the eight exams. I was not able to get to the first one. On the day of the second I slept late, but managed to get there in time. Outside the University were twenty police cars, but I slipped in with the crowd of students and did the exam. A friend passed a message across to me. 'The police are waiting for you. Come with me in my car.' I refused his offer as I did not want to make trouble for him. I managed to get out unseen and also to sit five more of the exams—making six in all. After 15 days the results came out: I had passed all six.

In September I went back home to Luxor. The streets were full of soldiers. I hid in a building and refused to leave. My friends supported me, but my father was threatened so I gave myself up to the police. I spent one night in the police station and they began by treating me rough, but I was very rude with them. The next day I was transferred to Assiut—it was a laugh—a crazy show. I was handcuffed and escorted by four soldiers with guns, like a murderer. There were 100 soldiers on the station and I was put in an empty carriage guarded by two soldiers and an officer. People on the station were shouting, encouraging me and throwing parcels of food. I was handcuffed to the seat all night. At Assiut a great Mercedes took me to the police station. I spent three nights there all alone in a dirty cell, which was flooded to keep me awake. I could only have a blanket to sleep from 2 a.m. to 6 a.m.

When I was taken before the judge to be questioned he had 75 pages of evidence against me. The judge questioned me on my opinions of the government's policy, on the US policy in Vietnam and on our dealings with Israel, and then he laughed and said that he could not let me leave––he had his orders.

The prison in Assiut was cleaner than the police station. I was held for two months, and then released after a decision from Sadat.

I went back to Luxor and took my degree, and then did my Masters' degree in Cairo University, but my thesis 'How to rule Egypt' was not accepted.

After this I did my 3 years' national service in the army. In spite of my past record I was made an officer. This ends the most interesting part of my life, and I was proud of it.

After I left the army I wanted a quiet life, so I think to marry. I found a girl and we became engaged. I was a teacher in a Commercial School at this time. I was not happy there for the teachers and the head were against me because I told students not to go to teachers' homes for 'private lessons'. It is a custom that if students want to do well in exams they pay for extra lessons at the teachers' house, otherwise they cannot do well. Where do students find this extra £5 a month? Their fathers are equally poor as teachers, why should the teacher have a colour television? All students were pushed into these private lessons, but I stayed behind at the school to help my students and did not ask them for money.

I had hoped that my girl was different from other Egyptian girls, but she was not. She wanted money for many many things. What should I do? Break it off or do what she wants? To earn extra money I worked at a hotel for 9 hours each day after I had done my 6 hours teaching. After a year I became ill. My girl said 'I didn't see you too much. . .' We had arguments and then we split up.

In 1981 I left the school and the hotel and started to handle tourist groups. I also worked to improve my English, and once more began to write seriously.

I love Egypt and I cannot leave. All I need is enough money for travel, books, friends and to care for my family. I pay 90% of the family expenses now and also put away £100 each month for my parents to make the pilgrimage to Mecca. They will need £4,000. I need to earn a lot. The average wage for someone with a degree is £60 per month, for someone with only a school education £40 per month. If you have no education at all and do manual work you can earn £5 a day, so you see education is not really respectable!

My wish is to finish with tourism and to start a bookshop, for Egyptians, and to write.

EL ASASIF

CHAPTER 11

'I must *do* something,' I said to Taha one morning in despair. 'I could sit here in the sun for ever watching people.'

'Hire a bicycle,' he suggested. 'Go exploring.'

'How much should I pay for an afternoon?'

'One pound, no more!'

In the back streets leading away from the river were several shops hiring bicycles and I found a machine with most of its faculties intact.

'How much to hire this for one afternoon?'

'Two pounds.'

'That is too expensive. I will go somewhere else.'

'Is very good bicycle. O.K. One pound fifty.'

'Still too much. Look, the saddle wobbles. The brakes are not too good either. I will give you one pound.'

'No. Is not possible.'

'Pity. Never mind. Goodbye.'

The shop owner looked at his watch.

'O.K. Is already near two o'clock. I let you have it for one pound.'

I wobbled off down the road very slowly. There was not much traffic, and it didn't seem to matter very much which side of the road I used.

When I felt I'd got some sort of control I went to the river and pushed the machine down through the sand to the jetty. The local ferry was waiting to cross, so handing over 10 piastres with confidence, (Taha told me it was 10, but if you ask the fare you are told that it's 20) I pushed the bike on to the steel deck—it was like stepping on to a hotplate. The ferry was a huge iron structure with a raised section at each end. The central area was filled with sacks, crates, bicycles and bodies. I was the only foreigner on board, as tourists usually use the Tourist Ferry further down the river.

As the ramp was winched up and the engine revved, last minute arrivals slithered down the bank and, with the hem of their gallabiyas held in their teeth, leapt dangerously aboard.

From the shore the Nile had looked dark, almost black, but once out on the water it was deep olive green, smooth and opaque.

The moment the ship touched the opposite bank there was a wild scramble as everybody tried to get off at once. Egyptians are very peaceful, relaxed people at all times except when getting on or off transport, when their natures change entirely. I held back until the worst was over and then, following a woman with an enormous brightly coloured bundle on her head, pushed the bike up the ramp.

Round the landing stage were unsavoury looking food and drink stalls, and yellow plastic bottle-crates were stacked beside the road. A country lane led straight inland between fields and palm groves towards the foot of the cliffs which rise over 1,000 feet at the edge of the Western Desert. The twisted pedals of my bike wove an eccentric design as they turned, and the road was rough, but somehow the machine held together.

All along the road I passed donkey carts, people walking and cycling, wildly hooting taxi-vans and children shuffling home from school carrying bundles of books tied together with string.

'Hello'.

'Good morning'.

'What your country? England? Good!'

On this side of the river the little boys were much cheekier. Two astride a load of sugar cane on a donkey cart called out:

'Egyptian zig-zig very good for you.'

I smiled and waved.

'Bokra, bokra!' (Tomorrow, tomorrow!) I called back, and they fell about with delighted giggles.

At the foot of the cliffs small villages nestled amongst the dry heaps of fallen rock. Living there must be like living in a hot gravel pit. Some of the houses were painted with pictures of trees, water, houses and, surprisingly, aeroplanes. I found out later that this indicated that the inhabitants had been on the pilgrimage to Mecca. Sometimes there was a painting of a red hand, to ward off the evil eye. Abdul had told me something about this during my Arabic lessons. He insisted that it was only the older folk who still believed in this power. He showed me a lump on his wrist.

'My mother is sure that this was due to the evil eye.'

'How is that?'

'When I passed all my examinations. She thinks it was caused by the jealousy of one of our neighbours.'

He also told me that there is a special word in Arabic meaning 'someone-a-long-way-off'. It has to be used in certain situations, such as when selling insurance. If a salesman were to say 'Supposing your house caught fire,' he would instantly be suspected of ill-wishing the house, but if he begins with 'Just supposing the house of someone-a-long-way-off were to catch fire . . .' then he is more likely to get a hearing.

The cliffs above the villages were honeycombed with dark openings. To the left a road led off to the Tombs of the Queens, to the right the Valley of the Kings was hidden up in the mountains. Alongside the road from the ferry were two immense seated stone figures. These were the Colossi of Memnon, gazing over the fields of sugar cane towards Luxor with blind battered eyes.

I cycled along the foot of the hills with bright green fields on my right and glaring hot tawny rock on my left. The line between desert and fertile land is precise and clear-cut. Groups of women in black were sitting at the roadside. The women looked tired and solemn, but when I called out 'Ma'a salaama' to some of them ('peace go with you') their faces brightened in the dark shadow of their black headcloths as they smiled and waved. Each tiny contact, I felt, was a bridge, thread-like but nevertheless real, between our two cultures.

Turning my back on the green fields I cycled up a road between the dry sandy cliffs and reached the mortuary temple of Queen Hatshepsut, who was a powerful ruler during the 15th century B.C. This is the only temple to a woman ruler in Egypt. Set back into the base of the cliffs, its clean horizontal lines and rows of pillars are so intact that, from a distance, it looks quite modern. The heat reflected by the cliffs was menacing, so after a brief pause in the shade of a Thomas Cook rest house, I turned back. It was a relief to cycle between the growing crops again. Squatting figures harvested bundles of clover for animal fodder, which they pulled out by hand. There was an intriguing squeaky rustling rising from a sugar-cane field, caused, I discovered, by a group of men pulling up the fat ten-foot canes and twisting off the shiny strap-like leaves. Lots of people on the road were chewing lengths of sugar cane—it looked awfully stringy stuff.

After I had crossed back to Luxor on the ferry, I went down to sit on a peaceful jetty away from the centre of the town. Graceful feluccas making their last trip of the day were silhouetted against the sky. The sun sent a golden path across the water and then, as it went behind the low dusty bands of cloud just above the horizon, the gold turned to red.

At this moment the surface of the water began to flicker with tiny fish jumping so fast as to tease the eyes; wherever I looked they had just disappeared. A big grey cow with black hood and wings plodded up and down on the brink inspecting the day's supply of interesting débris. The golden cliffs on the far side of the river turned quickly to silhouettes. I loved the smooth river, so truly a river of life, and longed for the next day when I would go to Aswan and see the water leap at the first cataract.

CHAPTER 12

A quiet knock at the bedroom door. When I opened it a sleepy boy whispered

'Five o'clock Madaam.'

I was up before the muezzin, and it was still dark. When I got down to the entrance hall of the hotel my breakfast was waiting for me on a tray, but the boy had gone back to sleep on the floor behind the reception desk. He must have slept there all night as there was an alarm-clock on the floor beside him. He roused himself up again and made me some tea, a great length of lad in a grubby white gallabiya and a long orange knitted cardigan with a khaki towel turbanned round his head. When I had finished eating he proudly showed me his books. One was a love story on limp paper with hearts, flowers, cupids and chastely kissing couples on each page.

'It is *lovely*,' he said dreamily. 'Boys and girls.'

Western-style love affairs are forbidden to Muslims. Courtship and marriage are still very formal. The other book was a two year old desk diary, published by some agricultural company. In the front (back!) he had carefully written his name and age, 18. He had seven names, two of which were Mahmoud. The diary contained weakly coloured pictures of farming scenes, one for each month. I admired every one.

He then locked the hotel and walked with me in the warm early morning darkness to the 'bus station.

'It is lovely now, before the sun' he smiled happily.

The 'bus was the usual tatty tin crate. On one front seat sat a dark-skinned old gaffer holding a newspaper packet in one hand. It oozed slightly, some substance rather like H.P. Sauce. He regularly cleared his throat and spat generously on the sandy floor.

The 'bus went round the town hooting stridently at significant points. Considering the fact that it was 6 a.m. and still dark there was a remarkable number of people about, including the usual small conference groups sitting cross-legged on the roadside. Outside a bakery a table was piled high with newly backed pitta bread, and the smell was mouth-watering. A donkey, pulling a flat cart loaded with loaves, pattered off down the street on its delivery round. My grey breakfast roll was still wedged aggressively between a couple of my ribs. Brown pitta bread is subsidised by the government, and so it is cheap in order to encourage the Egyptians to eat it. The less nutritious white (grey) bread is served to foreigners unless they specifically ask for Egyptian bread. That morning I had forgotten.

Lots more locals boarded the bus, and nearly everyone seemed to be carrying a cardboard box tied with string. By 6.30 we were away. The sky was pink and a range of jagged mountains like grey paper cut-outs lined the horizon to the east. On the right was the Nile, obscurred most of the way by a gravel bank, but beyond it the western mountains were pink and gold. A slimy canal followed the road on the left. The driver tooted and waved at the military checkpoints.

I was now alone in a 'bus full of utterly foreign and completely indifferent men. They were mostly old and rough-looking, and many were carrying sticks. I gradually realised that nobody at home knew where I was, and nobody here cared. The bus pushed through a creamy flock of camels on Esna Bridge, turned into the market place and stopped. There was not a European face in sight to appeal to—not even a pair of trousers. I was suddenly terrified. At the market stalls women in black, their metal teeth flashing, haggled shrilly over bundles of onions. They didn't look at all sympathetic. I hated Esna, a beastly mucky little town. Why did the bus park there for *so long*? I noticed that the old gaffer's newspaper packet was now one sticky mass of H.P. Sauce. I got out my notebook and wrote 'Please let's go now. I promise not to get itchy feet again.' I was rigid with tension, and for no particularly good reason. Nobody was taking any notice of me.

At last the bus groaned into action and squeezed between the stalls, donkeys and goats, and crossed the bridge again. Still tense as we drove on between banana plantations, I thought 'why on earth go *another* two hundred miles south for God's sake?' I concentrated on thoughts of home; things like sitting in front of a wood fire with a glass of whisky in my hand, a cat purring on my lap, talk of books and poetry. This worked, and I gradually calmed down.

Most of the villages were primitive mud-brick affairs until we got to Kom Ombo. There the houses we passed were still mud-brick, but nearly all were whitewashed and some had a bit of decorative brickwork or paintings on the walls. From Kom Ombo to Aswan the outlook brightened. By this time the gaffer's packet had disappeared. Had he dropped it? Thrown it out? Eaten it . . .?

Aswan was the smartest town I had yet seen. The Corniche sweeps along beside the Nile with almost decent pavements and a smooth dual carriageway. The smartness was only one block deep—behind was the usual fascinating maze of litter-strewn streets. The Nile was dotted with interesting islands made up of smooth lumps of rock which looked like groups of basking hippos. The long Elephantine Island lies opposite the town. The river was blue, and the white felucca sails everywhere made it feel almost Mediterranean.

The hotel where I'd been recommended to stay was full, so I went up-market a bit for a soft bed, just for once. The manager of the Kalabsha looked at my travel-worn clothes and asked for a £50 deposit to be paid in advance. He also took my passport. A fleet of superior Sultans, dressed in cream and brown robes, waited on the guests with supreme indifference. I managed, with difficulty, to coax an omelette and tea out of them.

After a welcome shower I had a long, long rest on the soft bed, easing my hips which were quite bruised from sleeping on hard ones. Then, in order to save any problems the next day, I walked to the railway station to buy my ticket for the return journey to Luxor. There was a queue. Eventually a man came to tell us that we could not buy tickets because the ticket staff were praying.

'Come back in one hour.'

An hour later I returned to be told that they had returned from praying, but were now sleeping.

'Come back at four o'clock.'

I returned at twenty past four, to avoid the queue, and was told

'Tickets finished now. Come tomorrow.'

'At what time?'

Seven thirty in morning.'

'*What?*'

'When your train?'

'Four o'clock in the afternoon.'

'Come at four o'clock. No problem'

I gave up, and went off to explore more of Aswan. A young American student with black hair and fair skin had also been trying to get a ticket. He shrugged and set off down the road beside me, telling me about his travels. His name was Pete and he was from Hawaii. He was making his way round the world and had come up to Egypt through Africa. The stories he told me made my journey sound like a picnic.

'Some countries—they're so poor they don't have no paper. None at all. You go to market to buy vegetables and have to carry them in your hands.'

He was down to his last few pounds and trying to get to Cairo before he ran out, so I treated him to a drink and a cake. Then we walked along to a park at the far end of the Corniche. While I sat on the grass, he lay along the top of a wall with his head on his rucksack telling me more about his travels and his home.

A Nubian came up, his skin ebony black against a yellow robe.

'This your father?' he asked, cheekily. I gave some lighthearted reply, but he kept on asking Pete silly questions and then started pushing at his shoulder. Pete suddenly lost his patience and flared up. Leaping off the wall he grabbed the Nubian boy by the shoulders and shouted

'You just leave me alone. Get it?'

The Nubian smiled and wandered off, quite untroubled. Pete was tired out as he'd had a long day, so he went off to the hostel where he was staying, and I went back to my hotel.

Sitting in the garden waiting for one of the Sultans to bring me a beer I heard hundreds of sparrows chattering in the bushes making a silvery torrent of very English sound. Suddenly the garden lights were switched on and there was total silence. The beer, when it came, was small, warm, flat and expensive. I thought longingly about Yorkshire bitter.

Later that evening I met Wendy, an American girl. She had flown down to Aswan, leaving her family staying with some friends in Cairo, and wanted to visit the High Dam and some of the sights on her own. Apparently they were very unwilling for her to do this, but had eventually agreed. I suggested that we might go together. The things she wanted to see were all quite far apart and we thought that it would make sense if we hired a car and split the cost. We agreed the plan—we would be real tourists for a day.

It was good to sleep between cotton sheets in a soft bed, just for one night, but none of the luxury made me as happy as when staying with my Egyptian friends.

CHAPTER 13

Having agreed a price with the driver, and written it down in his presence, Wendy and I were taken at 8 o'clock in the morning to a quarry near Aswan where an unfinished obelisk lies. It was originally intended to stand outside the temple of Queen Hatshepsut, but before the sculptors had finished cutting it out of the rock-face it cracked, so it was abandoned.

Wendy told me that the previous evening she had walked across the rocky waste land from the town to take a look at the quarry on her own, but had found the gates locked. She had had an unpleasant walk back to the town as darkness was falling, stumbling over rocks, débris and the occasional dead donkey.

We went in and stood on the obelisk whilst the guides filled our ears with statistics: It is 41.75 metres high, 4.2 metres square at the base and its estimated weight is 1,168 tons. The method of cutting out the obelisk was to pound at it with a round stone made of a harder rock. It was possible to see the rounded dents where the work had stopped in the 15th century B.C. Once more it was not the great size of the monument that I found moving, but the small marks of individual effort and workmanship.

Next we were taken across the old Aswan Dam to a jetty where we boarded a small boat to go to The Temple of Philae. In the bows sat a sinister figure in a long robe, his head and face completely wrapped against the fresh morning air, and his eyes hidden by dark glasses, which reflected the ripples of the water. The ferryman told us he was one of the attendants who worked on the island, but his stillness and anonymity made me think that perhaps he was one of the original priests of the temple come back to haunt us. If we had unpeeled the wrappings what would we have seen?

When the first dam was built in 1902, most of The Temple of Philae was submerged where it originally stood. When the new High Dam was being constructed in 1971, it was decided to move the temple, chunk by numbered chunk, to an island. It now looks as if it has always been there. We chugged across the black satiny water, round jagged promontories and islands until suddenly there it was, like a honey coloured prima-donna, admiring its sunlit reflection in the water.

We were given an hour to look round the temple, and as it was still early there weren't many visitors, so we felt as if it belonged to us. It was good to feel the sharply cut edges of the original carvings, unspoilt by time or immersion. The centuries had left many other carvings too: a visiting party of Frenchmen (Balzac, Rimbaud, Lenoir) had autographed the temple walls, and graffiti in many other languages and alphabets, although they should have aroused our disapproval, gave the place a sort of living continuity. One ancient one in Latin, stated that 'So-and-so (I forget the name) stultus est.' in other words '.....is a twit'. Nothing changes.

Next we were driven to the new High Dam. It is not so impressive to the eye as the name sounds, being so enormous that it is really a huge industrial area linking peninsulas and islands to block the river and provide hydro-electric power. The road along the top of the dam is bordered by trees and gardens. Here we stood, looking along Lake Nasser which sparkled away for nearly 200 miles between intricate rocky mounains to the border with the Sudan. It was a sad moment. There was no time to go further, but the south beckoned strongly, the panic of yesterday had evaporated. One day, one day . . .

After a visit to a rather gloomy museum which illustrated the history of the building of the dam, we were taken back to Aswan town with still a good part of the afternoon left. We walked along by the river, passing some boys who had been shooting sparrows, looking for the ferry which would take us across to Elephantine Island. A felucca boy eagerly offered to sail us across. His boat was spotlessly white with bright red and blue cushions and although it took him longer to unfurl his sail than to make the short journey, it was worth the trouble to see the pleasure on his face when we accepted his offer.

Elephantine Island is so called because of its humpy rocks, one of which looks just like an elephant's head. On the island are the ruins of an ancient Egyptian frontier fortress. An old guide found us wandering about in the ruins, and in a fast whispered mixture between English, Arabic and a sort of Esperanto told us indignantly how the Romans had come and smashed up the place to use the materials for their own buildings, which now in their turn also stood in ruins. He was difficult to understand, but fortunately he repeated things a lot, so we could get the idea on the second or third time round. He was obviously still, after all those years, pretty cross with the Romans. Padding ahead of us in his bare feet, the slender bent old man beckoned urgently for us to follow and see something special. Leading us round a fallen block he showed us with pride a relief sculpture of a god, a little of the original colour still showing. From the outstretched hands of the god the water of the Nile poured. The old man sighed with pleasure.

Lastly he showed us the Nilometer. This is where steps lead down through the rock to the water, and each side on the walls scales of measurement are engraved in Greek, Roman, Arabic and Pharaonic to show the depth of the water. The water level that day was well below the lowest mark.

We left our gentle guide with a handsome tip and many thanks and then went to visit a nearby garden full of bright exotic flowers. Brilliant butterflies followed us under canopies of crimson and gold blossoms. An energetic little man with gaping baggy trousers and gappy teeth to match, rushed us from shrub to shrub telling us their names and what they were used for. Scents of crushed basil and lemon balm rose intoxicatingly in the heat. He cradled unopened buds lovingly between his hands crying:

'Babies! Babies!' and then clapped his hands with excitement.

'Good-see, good-see! Lilies, Lilies. Good-see, good-see Yasmine. Drinkee-tee, drinkee-tee, yes, yes.'

Still clapping excitedly he led us to an uninteresting green shrub.

'Hen-na, hen-na. Lovely ladies, ladies, yes, yes.' He mixed an imaginary handful and spread it on his beaming, bristly face.

'Good-see, good-see Christmas,' indicating poinsettias that shone like flames. His enthusiasm was infectious and, unlike most guides, he gave no hint of wanting a tip. At his request I took a picture of him with Wendy.

'I reckon a copy of that will mean more to him than a tip,' she said, for he had proudly shown us crumpled photos sent to him by previous visitors. I made a note of his name and promised to send him a copy.

In the centre of the garden was a circular lattice-work summer house weighed down with jasmine. The sinewy stem of the tree twisted right through the wall like a vine. As we sat in the fragrant shade, we were served with tea. Just as we were about to sip, the little gardener rushed in with sprigs of sweet mint which he rammed into our glasses with grubby fingers. It was delicious.

We left the garden reluctantly and walked through a nearby Nubian village. The Nubians, unlike the majority of Egyptians, are almost totally black. They were friendly, too friendly somehow, beckoning us into their houses. Some of the children asked us for money, but although the village was primitive, nobody looked hungry, and there was no lack of television sets in the dark mud-brick houses.

We stroked two tiny goats which were only a day or two old with black silky coats and wobbly legs. White egrets paced round the rubbish-dumps. We felt that we were being watched, and the atmosphere of the village made us uncomfortable, so we slithered down the brown dusty banks to the shore to catch the ferry which was just coming in.

Back at the hotel Wendy and I parted company and, collecting my rucksack, I went to the station to catch the train back to Luxor. I had no trouble whatever buying my ticket as nobody was sleeping or praying at that particular moment. The only incident on the journey was the sight of a momentary flash of movement amongst the litter under one of the seats. Was it something alive, or was it just the light flickering?

At Luxor the train was too long for the platform so, encouraged by another passenger who said that this was definitely the thing to do, I dropped the four feet or so from the carriage door on to the track amongst the signal cables and points, and scrambled up the embankment into town.

The regrets at having to resist the lure of the south were soon overshadowed by the welcome familiarity of Luxor. Now that I was going north my intermittent nervousness had completely gone and I was beginning to be able to 'read the people'. Sounds of singing and drumming came from the cafés near the station. The night was warm, and as I strolled along by the river towards my hotel a voice shouted.

'Hello, welcome. You have a good time in Aswan?'

It was Ibrahim whom I had met in the Savoy Hotel gardens the previous week. Further along the road another voice called:

'Welcome back. Come and have a drink. Tell me about Aswan.'

This time it was Taha. We sat under the trees outside the Luxor Hotel, and the waiter brought us some warm beer.

'How you like Aswan?' asked the waiter. 'Better than Luxor, yes?'

'Aswan was beautiful,' I replied, 'but Luxor feels like home.'

CHAPTER 14

The welcomes continued well into the following day. Ali called out from his felucca:

'Hello Engleesh. You like Aswan?' I went to have a last talk to him, as I was leaving for Cairo that night. He introduced me to his friend Faruz, who had a gleaming metal tooth, and they invited me to come back and have tea with them later.

At the hotel the boy with the seven names took all the clothes that I was not wearing to wash them. Later I saw him pounding them with a long pole in an aluminium tub four-feet wide in the back kitchen, (so that's how it is done!) and everything was returned to me in the evening, clean, dry and perfectly ironed. Even my socks had been neatly pressed and folded. Nobody would take any money for doing it.

In the restaurant that evening the big African cook came out of his kitchen to chat. His small assistant, his vest hanging out as usual, stood two paces behind him, beaming. When I had finished eating, the cook, pointing to the lad, said:

'This nigger here, he want give you tea. He pay.'

A tray of tea was brought, and they stood by making sure that I enjoyed it.

The train for Cairo left at 1 a.m. and was scheduled to reach Cairo by noon the next day. Staying awake until one o'clock was a problem. The hotel manager insisted that I could use my room to relax in, although the bed was already made up for the next guest.

From ten o'clock onwards I sat in the tiny foyer with the porter watching his portable television. From time to time his friends called in to see him and tea would be brewed. There was always a cup for me. At midnight I was stiff with sitting, so I shouldered my rucksack, shook hands with everyone, and left to wander down through the mediaeval back streets to the station.

I felt safe even in the murkiest of lanes, and the only approaches that anyone made were friendly and helpful. There are, of course, attacks and murders committed in Egypt, but almost invariably they will be due to family feuds. As one Egyptian author put it: 'Why should we care enough about a stranger to kill him?' Women, with their special position in Muslim society, are further protected. Yes, it has to be said, Luxor at night felt a lot safer than most English cities.

In the square by the station a few horse-drawn carriages were waiting patiently for the next train to arrive. The drivers were having drinks at the nearby tea stalls, and their untethered horses stood munching at piles of bright green clover. Dogs were scavenging in the shadows on the railway track. In the entrance hall of the station an old man was beginning to wash the large area of white marble floor with a dishcloth and a small bucket. It must have taken him all night to do it. A cheerful bonfire burned on the pavement opposite the station steps where I stood and watched the lovely, scruffy place. The air was like silk. I didn't want to leave.

A well dressed young man came up and announced:

'I am a graduate from the Faculéty of Arts, and I would like to speak to Your Majesty for (he consulted his watch) a quarter of an hour.'

There was nothing else to do, so I listened while he told me all about himself and his life. Now that his studies were over he was going to Cairo to do his National Service.

'I am exciting talking to you. I will sit by you in the train and talk all night.'

At this I had to say a firm No. I wandered off and found a nice polished granite slab to lie on, with my head on my rucksack, enjoying the warm night.

The first class carriage was dirty but comfortable, with roomy reclining seats amply upholstered. I managed to sleep for short stretches. In one interval of wakefulness again I thought I saw a movement under the seat opposite. I kept perfectly still and a small grey mouse emerged, sat up amongst the pile of litter and nibbled a crust between its paws. As the night wore on I was conscious of other small livestock, this time it was First Class Fleas taking their nourishment.

By eight o'clock the next morning we had only got as far as Assiout. While I was standing in the corridor for a change of position an old soldier shuffled by. He touched my face gently, distressed by the mosquito-bites I had suffered in Luxor. Later a man came along with a newspaper, and stopping just beyond me he opened it and spread it on the floor. He took off his watch and placed it on the paper. Then after removing his shoes, he knelt on the paper, facing towards the east, and prayed. It is said that if a woman stands behind a man who is praying, it is as good as praying herself, so I did.

A fair haired girl in jeans came along the corridor with a cine camera, and as we passed through a particularly primitive village she opened the door and leaned out, whirring efficiently. The waiter was passing and stopped.

'Is not allowed. Shut the door.'

Giving him a look which all but said 'Get stuffed!' she continued filming. He tried again to stop her, but she ignored him and continued to gobble the poverty of his country into her camera.

'Why do you English take pictures of these *dirty* things,' Abdul said to me when I got back to Leeds and showed him my pictures. The one that had upset him was of a meek donkey pulling a small cart.

'This is a *rubbish* cart—why did you take a picture of this?'

'I'm sorry,' I said, 'but I do like donkeys.' He shrugged crossly.

There were no meals provided on this train, only tea and dry grey bread rolls with cheese. I saw the waiter put his tray of rolls on the floor while he went into the lavatory. Having seen the state of that particular lavatory I went without a cheese roll, and by the time the train had found its way into Cairo five hours late, I had been without food for 24 hours.

In Luxor I had asked Taha about the problem of gifts. Egyptians are very good at giving, but when receiving a gift they give it scant attention, and put it aside. I wanted to give something to the Sawy family to express my thanks for their hospitality, but didn't want to offend them.

'I know I can't give money, although I'm sure they haven't much,' I said.

'No, no,' said Taha. 'Not money. I don't know. Some chocolates maybe. . .'

When I went for my Arabic lessons in Leeds I used to tape-record each lesson so that I could go over it again later. One week I forgot to take a blank tape with me, so Abdul gave me one. The following week I gave him a tape to replace it.

'What is this?' he said.

'To replace the one you gave me,' I said. He looked almost irritated.

'But that was a gift,' he insisted. Seeing my embarrassment he continued:

'This giving of something in return, in Egypt we call it the "British Way".'

'This "British Way",' I said, 'is it good, or bad?'

He paused, and then said gently, 'It is very—aah—*correct*!'

I puzzled over the problem on the local train out of Cairo, and then decided to take Taha's advice. When I reached the suburb, I bought a huge box of chocolates for the family. I was given a marvellous welcome home. My gift was accepted quietly and put away, but it came out later in the evening and everyone *looked* as if they were enjoying them . . .

CHAPTER 15

I managed with difficulty to extract myself, in Arabic, from the family in the morning.

'I go Cairo. Bank. Airline Office. Buy gifts my children. I go alone. O.K?'

Zeinab and Om Saabir, who were having a noisy exchange on the landing, shook their heads and tut-tutted, but they let me go. I wanted to experience Cairo in daylight on my own, and also I didn't want the boys to spend any more time and money on me.

As I suspected, distances in the centre of the city were shorter on foot than they seemed to be in the buses, which spend more time snarled up in traffic-jams than actually moving. I found one good book shop, which used up a lot of time, and then after tea and a cake in a tea-shop, went to a bank which displayed a 'Visa Card' sign, to draw some money for a few gifts to take home.

It was first necessary to queue up to draw the money from one desk in dollars. An old woman in front of me was signing a thousand dollars' worth of travellers' cheques. When she had finished, and then had leafed through them again slowly to check that she hadn't missed any, I was at last given a form to fill in. I handed it in together with my card and was told to wait for three quarters of an hour. When I came back I was handed the money in dollars, which I then had to take to the currency exchange desk to convert into Egyptian currency.

'Why you want this money?' asked the official behind the desk.

'To spend of course. What a silly question.'

'No! No! Is *not* a silly question,' he snapped back, but exchanged the money without asking anything further.

During my explorations I learned something else about the skinny little soldiers with the big boots. I came across a crowd of them sitting side by side along a low wall waiting for something or other. All their feet hung down in a row, but it definitely seemed to me that *every pair of boots was the same size.*

The sky was overcast, and the gritty heat didn't encourage much further exploration of the city, so I took the train back to the Sawy's house. As I went up the stairs I heard Ali's plaintive voice calling out from the bathroom:

'Mayya! Mayya!' (Water, water.) The water supply had been cut off and he couldn't have a shower. Hussein was leaning over the balcony holding out a small plastic plate.

'What are you doing?'

'Water, for Ali,' he grinned, looking up at the sky. A few big drops of rain fell for a minute or two, but they all missed his plate. That is about all the rain they ever get in Cairo.

When Omar came home from work and we had eaten, he offered to take me to the Islamic part of Cairo where there are many mosques. Near the Hussein Mosque there is a network of small streets called the Khan el Khalili Market which I also wanted to see. As we drew near to this area the crowds in the road became almost solid. An unbroken sea of turbans bobbed in front of the bus. Brightly coloured neon strips dangled from the buildings, stalls lined the streets, and even the Hussein Mosque itself flashed and sparkled like a Christmas tree. It was the feast of Hussein—we had chosen the right day to come. When we got off the bus we were immediately caught up in a vigorous scrum, pushing and shoving with hands and elbows. Omar told me to hold his arm tightly. Policemen made vague attempts to keep a two-way flow, but the crowd was having a good time and took no notice.

'Hold your money,' shouted Omar, but although a thousand hands seemed to be on me at once as we squeezed along I felt no thieving fingers. Every now and then a gang of lads arm-in-arm would hurl themselves forward against the flow and cause a flare-up of shouting and some battered shins. My feet trod on God knows what (or who) as we staggered through to the narrow market streets where the crowd was slightly thinner.

We wandered into shops which sold intricate gold and silver dishes and trays, boxes decorated with mother-of-pearl, jewellery and leather goods. Spice stalls gave off intriguing smells and pungent smoke from incense-burners poured up into the darkness. Great golden mountains of 'hummus' (chick-peas) were everywhere, and the stall holders poured them about shouting to people to buy. Murky cafés stood on every corner, the battered wooden chairs spilling out on to the pavement. They all seemed to be full of men.

'All men, men, men,' I shouted to Omar, and it certainly seemed to be so. Men embracing each other, walking arm in arm or hand in hand laughing, teasing, pushing, wearing paper hats, playing finger-cymbals, drumming drums. A few women and children picked their way in and out, and occasionally two or three girls came along together, holding each other tightly.

'Boys with boys, girls with girls, but no boys with girls,' I commented.

'That's right,' said Omar. However although he and I, arm in arm, were unique in this respect, everyone was far too busy to take any notice of us.

We sat outside a corner café to rest and watch the crowd. At this spot a wrought-iron barrier eight-feet high runs down the centre of the road separating the two lanes. Excited figures, robes flapping, were constantly scrambling over it, too impatient to walk round.

'Country people,' said Omar. 'They go mad when there is feast.'

We ordered tea and the waiter dragged a tiny table over to us. The dented brass top was about ten inches square, and it wobbled dangerously on the cobbles on its long iron legs. It was more like a flower-pot stand than a table. The tea, served in glasses encrusted with tea-leaves and sugar, was hot, sweet and fragrant. Omar ordered a shisha (hookah) and sat smoking contentedly. The shisha has a mouthpiece like a metal ball with a hole in it. The waiter gives it a wipe with a grimy paw as he hands it over. The mouthpiece is mounted on a straight wooden pipe covered with cloth, which leads to a long rubber tube attached by another wooden pipe to the body of the machine. The water bubbles in the glass base as you draw the smoke through. On the top of the glass base is a brass candlestick-like structure and on the top of that sits a small earthenware cup full of sticky coarse tobacco with glowing charcoal balanced on top. As you draw, the coals burn brightly. I had a puff or two and the smoke tasted pleasantly clean for having been drawn through the water.

A small girl of about ten came past selling little booklets containing extracts from the Koran. Omar called her over and gave her a coin. She gave us a booklet, and then kissed the coin and put it into her pocket.

After this we pushed our way out through the crowd and, in preference to the bus, began to walk towards home. On the way we went to see Nasser's tomb. There is a mosque with a covered cloister along one side where his white marble tomb stands. Wreaths and flags were ranged behind it, and fresh flowers covered the top. He is remembered with much love by the Egyptians. Inside the building is a long carpeted room with formal chairs and tables grouped round. On the wall hangs a portrait of Nasser whose eyes seem to follow you wherever you go. Framed extracts from the Koran hang on the walls, and also the black velvet funeral pall, thickly embroidered with gold. At the far end of the room are a settee, three armchairs and a table from his palace. Some Egyptian ladies were exclaiming over them with wonder, and sitting down reverently. To me they looked like ordinary oldish brown velvet armchairs, but then I realised that most of the Egyptian houses that I had been in have either upright wooden chairs or hard divans.

We walked on through the quiet suburbs until we came to the district where the Sawy family used to live. Omar showed me a gap in the buildings overgrown with weeds.

'This was our home,' he said sadly, looking up to where the zig-zag line of a staircase could be seen on the wall, and patches of pink plaster still clung. He was happy there, and seemed to greet old friends on every corner. We called to see a close friend who was just about to leave his house as he was a player in a group called 'The eyes of Egypt' which performs at a smart hotel on the Giza road. With Egyptian hospitality he insisted that we drank a Coca Cola with him while he put on his bow-tie and adjusted his cummerbund.

Eyes are very significant to Egyptians and are mentioned in many sayings, phrases and compliments. If you say you will do something 'over my eyes,' you mean that you will do the task even if it costs you your eyes to perform it. Once Omar offered me his eyes. I accepted them solemnly and pretended to pocket them, which made him laugh.

In the next street we were hailed by one of Omar's many 'uncles' who ran a small kiosk. We were made welcome, invited to sit down on the pavement to talk and given further drinks, payment for which was refused of course. A tiny girl tottered past us in wet trousers. 'Uncle' called her over, told her to shake my hand, and then gave her a toffee, patted her mop of black curls and sent her on her way.

Out last call was to the telephone office to call England. This time we didn't have to wait long, and I soon came out of the office to meet up with Omar on the steps. It was so lovely to talk to my own family again that I went leaping down the road at his side, crazy with happiness.

'You happy, me happy,' he said.

We stopped at a stall and Omar bought glasses of hot hummus made from chick-peas garlic and lemon. A warming and nourishing drink. A spoon is provided to shovel out the soft peas at the bottom of the glass.

'You spend too much money on me,' I protested. 'You will have nothing left.'

'I have money—I happy. I have no money—I still happy,' said Omar. Unanswerable.

Back at the flat Father sat in his usual place on the divan, with his elbows resting on a thin cushion which he had placed on the table, his hands supporting his grizzled head. Whenever he saw me come home his face would pucker up into a wide toothless smile. He didn't say much, but it was usually something like 'marhab' (welcome) or 'Mapzuuta?' (happy?) or else something about being sad when I have to go away. One day I asked Ali his father's age.

'Is fifty-two,' replied Ali.

'But that is not possible,' I replied. 'That is only five years older than me.'

Ali looked wise and replied 'Ahh, but too much cigarettes and whisky when he young.' Was he pulling my leg again?

There was certainly plenty of smoking still going on in the flat, but definitely no drinking. I tried to imagine Ali's smooth, handsome countenance as wrinkled as his father's in twenty years' time—no, it was not possible.

We went downstairs for a late night cup of tea, and met another aunt. She was round and plump, and had a single tooth which signalled energetically as she talked. She took a great fancy to me and sat embarrassingly close. Through Ali, because she couldn't speak English, she demanded that I should make them a cake, an English cake. It was like the washing episode all over again. Total amnesia set in, and I couldn't remember anything about how I made an English cake. This time I was not going to risk making a fool of myself, so I pleaded tiredness and retired early to bed, reflecting wryly on how far my western 'freedom' had removed me from the rôle of the traditional home-maker and mother-figure who could make a cake blindfold. Now I was someone with a company to run, a hefty mortgage and an insatiable appetite for travel and writing.

CHAPTER 16

Against the background noise of a typical Cairo morning I worked hard to bring my notes up to date.

As well as the constant noise of hooting traffic, radios playing an assortment of popular Egyptian music blared out from the open windows as the local women got on with their housework. A strident megaphone was instructing a roaring crowd of children at a nearby school. The hammering in nearby workshops provided a rhythmic background to the eternal roadworks at the end of the street. Dogs barked, cats fought, chickens on a nearby roof squawked and the cockerel kept thinking it was dawn.

It was strange; at home the slightest noise is distracting, but this background was strangely soothing and a lot of work got done. Zeinab was, as always, preparing a meal in her kitchen, and periodically came to show me, with gestures and sign language, some culinary secret. That morning she was cooking some cauliflower. She boiled it until it was just tender, then dipped each head into a bowl of egg beaten up with flour and a handful of some bright green herb. Then she deep-fried the heads and we had them hot, and later, cold. Both ways were equally delicious. Zeinab used a lot of interesting herbs and we both felt the lack of an adequate dictionary when discussing cookery.

I refused all offers of hospitality from neighbours during the morning in order to get my work done. I was beginning to suffer from People-fatigue. Being the centre of interest and attention so much of the time was exhausting, and my energies were winding down. I had a promised visit with Yasmin to her University to cope with in the afternoon, and the prospect of shaking yet more hands and smiling was daunting.

At two o'clock, Uncle Yusef took us, Yasmin radiant and excited, to her University. We went in through a gateway to a tree-shaded area surrounded by dusty buildings, and Yasmin began to introduce me to her friends in the Faculty of English. The girls were charming, but their handshakes were universally limp and their conversation a series of flowery compliments which I began to find diffcult to stomach. The boys were courteous, intelligent, and keen to ask questions. They wanted to know about education in Britain, our way of life, my opinions on questions of progress, and my opinion of Egypt. They were critical of the Egyptian system of education, which still relies heavily on learning by rote. They were interested that I was writing about their country, and two of them took my address, saying that they would write to me.

One of the most difficult letters I had to answer later said:

'Here in Egypt, all the Egyptian are fond of football games, so, we watched the game between the Italian team (Jouvintos) and the English team (Liverpool) on the occasion of Europe's cup, but this game gave us a bad impression about the way of encouragement which the English people behave. We all saw how they were so cruel, merciless and hard-hearted with the Italian people, who were encouraging their team, before the beginning of the game, and it is not the first time in which they encroach and kill many innocent people without any sin.

But all Egyptian were so happy by the wise decision, which the Prime Minister in England took, 'Margaret T.' to punish this team and people who were the reason of that dreadful event, but I want to know what was the comments of the English newspapers and the public opinion on that events, and what is your own opinion of that characteristic of English people?'

I sat in on a history lecture, not understanding a word. The Professor droned on, occasionally rising to write a significant word on the blackboard. The students were serious and attentive, making notes and asking questions. The room was just a large hall filled with chairs. There were bookshelves on one side, but no books in them. Some of the windows were broken, and all the surfaces in the room were covered with a thin layer of sand.

Afterwards we went for tea in another room, and a loud-mouthed boy sidled up and started stroking my face, asking my age and trying to make me 'go with him'. My friends were shocked and apologised for him, but when I referred to the incident later at home, Yasmin affected not to remember it.

At last it was time to leave. With Yasmin and her friend clinging possessively to my arms, we walked home to the flat, the girls stopping at every shop to exclaim over the goods in the windows. I was completely exhausted when we got back, but the ordeal was not over. A visit to Ahmed, the eldest son, who lived on the far side of Cairo with his wife and five children was scheduled for the evening.

There were more new faces, food, drink, jokes, photographs that night. Ahmed's neighbours were invited in to share the fun, and in the end Ahmed and his wife begged me to stay the night. I nearly wept at the prospect. I'd had enough. Omar could see how I felt, so he made courteous excuses for me and we got away. In the dark we picked our way through the rotting debris, squelching overflows, boulders and mud of this newly-developed area. We clambered across the Cairo-Alexandria railway track by the light of flares illuminating the cart of an orange seller, and got into a bus for home. Naturally, Omar insisted on paying the fare, but I felt that the time had come to take a firm stand.

'Tomorrow is my last day, and tomorrow I pay. O.K?'

I said it with such ferocity, caused by both exhaustion and overburdened conscience that he agreed with hardly a murmur.

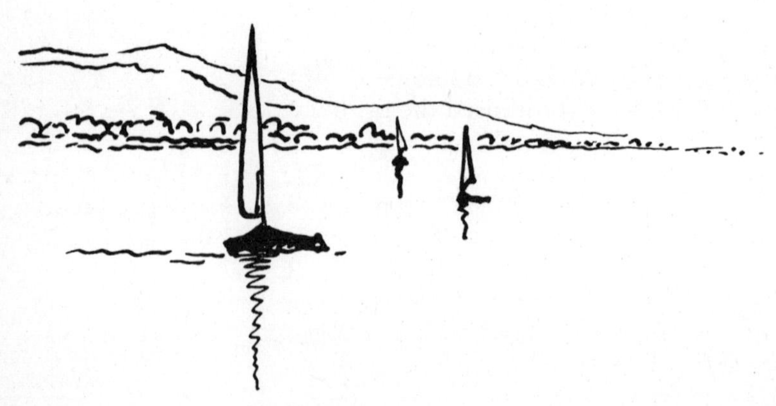

CHAPTER 17

Omar, Hussein and I arranged to go out at ten o'clock. Naturally we didn't. Everybody slept late. Zeinab went to market early and came home with five loofahs and about two tons of herbs for me to deliver to Sara in England. These were all packed into a big zip-up bag with much hilarity. Then Ali unpacked them all and undid all the bags of herbs for me to smell each one and learn its name and use. Zeinab kept asking 'Fi London?' (In London?') She can't remember, however often the boys tell her, that London and England are two different things, but is always interested to know whether, in England, we use any of the same things in cooking.

When discussing food with Abdul in Leeds he had told me that he and Sara never went out for a meal while they were in England. They were afraid that they would eat things which were forbidden to Muslims. He was an expert on English packeted and tinned foods and their contents, and constantly amazed at how much sugar we eat.

'In tins of peas, beans, even soup you have sugar,' he said incredulously. 'Why so much sugar?'

The day I gave Abdul and Sara some chocolates there was a tense moment or two while he scrutinised the list of ingredients on the box to make sure there was no animal fat included.

Once when they came to visit us he said he would like a fresh chicken to take back to Leeds, as they didn't like frozen ones. We called at a farm on the way back, and he selected a couple. The farmer was just about to wring their necks when Abdul stopped him.

'No, is not allowed,' and took the hens alive, sitting quietly in a sack, to the Leeds flat. I didn't stay to see what happened next, but Muslim law insists that all animals killed for meat must have their throats cut and bleed to death.

After I had smelt all the herbs Omar had to re-pack them, as Ali is so impractical. We squashed all the loofahs in too, and then added three more for my family.

Just as we were about to leave I heard Ali whisper to Omar something about 'enough money. . .?' 'My friend pays today,' Omar replied softly in Arabic, and Ali nodded. It is the custom for members of a family to help each other out with money. Often everyone will subscribe towards a big expense, such as buying a house, for one member of the family, then when that is paid off, someone else's turn will come.

The air in Cairo was dark again. Sand was blowing about like a brown fog and my nose started streaming. The boys took me to the Citadel, which is built on the slope of the Mokattam Hills on the east side of the city. It began as a fortress, built in the 12th century with stones taken from small pyramids at Giza. Later it was used as the official residence of the Sultans. In the early 18th century Mohammed Ali rebuilt and enlarged the Citadel and added the mosque which bears his name. On the outside the mosque is a delicate mass of domes and minarets, and the walls are covered with alabaster. Inside it is spacious and hung with lights made up of dozens of crystal balls suspended from huge rings which hang from the domes on unbelievably long chains. The domes are decorated inside with classical designs in dark green, gold and red. Concealed behind an ornate trellis screen is the tomb of Mohammed Ali. At the sanctuary end of the mosque, gold doors stand at the foot of a staircase up to the 'pulpit'. Apart from this the carpeted mosque is virtually empty. Other visitors, mostly Egyptians, were busy talking and taking photographs of each other, which seemed rather disrespectful.

The rest of the Citadel area looked like a building site, for it was being renovated. A garden-museum was being laid out where carved stone exhibits were placed individually in grassy areas, and there were seats and arbours being built for visitors.

The view of the city from the Citadel walls was wonderful that day, with the domes and minarets of some of its 500 mosques rising mysteriously out of the swirling sand-storm. The backdrop of tower blocks in the modern centre of the city was mercifully invisible.

Hussein spotted a pretty girl walking with her family. She caught his eye and separated from her family. They walked side by side talking to each other and Omar and I tactfully went on ahead and climbed about irresponsibly on the ramparts for a while. A little later the girl's family reclaimed her and they left the Citadel. Hussein returned to us, smiling ruefully.

'That's that,' he shrugged, resigned to the inevitable.

To cheer him up we went down from the Citadel to a pancake house. There was sawdust on the floor, and a few tables and chairs. Behind the counter a man was making a long sausage of white dough into balls the size of apples. A small boy, oily up to the elbows, took the balls, rolled them in oil and put them in rows on trays to rise. As each tray was filled he covered it with a grubby cloth. We ordered, and the man took a ball and rolled it flat. Then he tossed and twirled it in the air between his hands until the flying circle of dough was so thin that it was almost transparent. He then spread it with jam, coconut and raisins, folding it over between layers. He whisked it on to a hot griddle-iron where it cooked in a couple of minutes, and then sprinkled it with sugar. The small boy, meanwhile, took a filthy dishcloth and wiped our table down. Then he wiped a plate with the same cloth and slipped the hot pancake on to it. I fervently hoped that the heat from the pancake would sterilise the plate. It was cut into eight and presented with a flourish.

After we had finished, a tin mug on the table was filled from the tap by the small boy, and offered to each of us in turn to drink. I pleaded for tea, and the boy was sent down the street. Moments later an old man shuffled in with a tray.

Feeling satisfactorily full we walked back into the centre of the city through an area which specialised in furniture-making. The style of chair which many Egyptians favour has curved gilt legs, ornately carved, with upholstered seats of crimson satin or velvet. Piles of legs in various stages of completion were stacked outside the workshops down the street, and rolls of gaudy materials stood ready.

We reached home tired, coughing and sneezing and filthy. After another meal, I began to feel very shaky and was put to bed early with hot tea and aspirin. At about eleven o'clock I let out a wild yell. Omar and Ali rushed in. I had looked at my digital watch, and the date it showed was the 18th, the day I was meant to fly home.

'No, no. is O.K.,' they calmed me down. Omar brought in the calendar from the living-room wall. It showed both Arabic and English numerals.

'Today 17th—see.' Omar tore off that day's date and gave it to me to hold. After some careful thought I realised that my watch must have decided to change its date before midnight. Everything was fine.

The last morning. The family was unusually quiet. After breakfast Omar found some music on the radio and slowly began to dance. His slender body, dressed all in pale blue, bent and waved like a flower in the wind. The family clapped softly and tried to make me dance too, but I couldn't – his movements were too perfect, too expressive to emulate.

As I went down the stairs for the last time, Zeinab leaned over the rail with tears pouring down her cheeks, clutching the hem of her white headcloth. The car bounced away over the stones and we looked back to see the fluttering and waving until we turned the corner.

At the airport we sat in a row silently, until the flight was called. Hussein clasped his hands between his knees and bent his head. Omar's face, usually so merry, was grave and his dark eyes looked even larger than usual. I was reminded of this moment when weeks later I received a letter from him which began:

[IN THE NAME OF GOD]

Dear Joe, or the second mother . . .

Time to go. We shook hands solemnly, and I promised to return. Then as the plane rose and the sand swirled in the slipstream I could control myself no longer and hid my face.

I was sad to be leaving, and yet longing to be home. It didn't make sense. Yes it did. It is all about loving. There are so many loves. The Textbook decrees that you love your spouse and your children, respect your parents and do the best you can with your Neighbour. So much has to be learned and experienced in order to expand that into a full appreciation of what life really has to offer: a stream of tranquillity which, like the Nile, will always flow.

A THOUGHT OF THE NILE

It flows through old hushed Egypt and its sands,
Like some grave mighty thought threading a dream,
And times and things, as in that vision, seem
Keeping along it their eternal stands, –
Caves, pillars, pyramids, the shepherd bands
That roamed through the young world, the glory extreme
Of high Sesostris, and that southern beam,
The laughing queen that caught the world's great hands.

Then comes a mightier silence, stern and strong,
As of a world left empty of its throng,
And the void weighs on us; and then we wake,
And hear the fruitful stream lapsing along
Twixt villages, and think how we shall take
Our own calm journey on for human sake.

Leigh Hunt (1832)

"Perfection never strikes twice in the same place."

'Slow Boats Home' Gavin Young